500

white wines

500

white wines

the only white wine compendium you'll ever need

Natasha Hughes & Patricia Langton

SELLERS
PUBLISHING

A Quintet Book

Published by Sellers Publishing, Inc.
161 John Roberts Road, South Portland, Maine 04106
For ordering information:
(800) 625-3386 Toll Free
(207) 772-6814 Fax
Visit our Web site: www.sellerspublishing.com
E-mail: rsp@rsvp.com

ISBN: 978-1-4162-0771-9
Library of Congress Control Number: 2009923850
QTT.WWIN

This book was conceived, designed, and produced by
Quintet Publishing Limited
6 Blundell Street
London N7 9BH
United Kingdom

Project Editor: Martha Burley
Designer: Dean Martin
Art Director: Michael Charles
Managing Editor: Donna Gregory
Publisher: James Tavendale

10 9 8 7 6 5 4 3 2 1

Printed in China by SNP Leefung Printers Ltd.

contents

introduction

Grapevines have grown wild for thousands of years. Grape seeds dating back 8,000 years have been found in the Central European area now known as Georgia, while winemaking has certainly been practiced for 5,000 years. Tombs of the pharaohs of Ancient Egypt were decorated with scenes of vines and winemaking, and the Romans even had a textbook to teach viticulture to their newly conquered populations.

Wine is much more than just a drink. Through the centuries it has been traded across borders, and it has been present at treaties between nations and the coronations of kings. The fame of a region can rest on the quality of its wines. Making ordinary wine is easy, but making great wine is a constant challenge, balancing the effects of soil, sunshine, rain, and frost, along with the grape variety, its method of cultivation, and the skill of the winemaker.

Wine reflects the place where it is grown. It captures aspects of the soil and the weather in its flavor. This is known as the terroir. This explains why two wines, made from the same grape variety in different parts of the world, taste different. Wine also captures the essence of the grapes, their rich fruity flavors, the acidity, and the structure, which evolve over time.

When you begin to look closely at wine, it becomes more than just a drink

There is a wide range of wines covered in this book—varying in flavor, price, and origin

wine selection

With thousands of wine producers in dozen of countries making wines to stack on the shelves of stores and supermarkets, selecting the right wine to go with a simple supper, a grand dinner, or a special occasion can be daunting. This book aims to steer you toward the best wines from around the world, by describing the wine-growing regions, the grapes, and the climate of each, and then selecting some of the best winemakers, their vineyards, and wines in each area. It is a book that demands no previous knowledge of wine while it takes you on a journey of discovery.

The wines selected are not necessarily the most expensive, but they all have one thing in common—flavor for money. The combination of good grapes and the skill of the winemaker to create fine-tasting wine at whatever price point the occasion demands has been the ultimate criterion for inclusion in this book. While most producers have just one wine listed, the fact that they are included in the book means that they have the ability to make exceptional wines. If you want to explore the world of wine beyond the 500 wines listed, the winemakers featured here are a good place to start.

Prices are indicated by bottle signs, (see price code box, right), which are an approximation only. International currency variations, taxes, and shipping costs may make a wine slightly cheaper or slightly more expensive in your area, but the general rule is that the more expensive wines have more bottle symbols.

Price code
▮ – wines up to $20
▮▮ – wines up to $30
▮▮▮ – wines up to $40
▮▮▮▮ – wines up to $50
▮▮▮▮▮ – wines over $50

how to use this book

Numbered circles on the map refer to the locations of the vineyards

An opening paragraph offers an overall description of the area, including the terrain of the region and the most popular grape varieties. It may also give a brief history of wine production in the region

Each wine comes with quick food pairing ideas for the perfect culinary experience

Touraine

Touraine's best whites come from Vouvray and Montlouis and are made from Chenin Blanc in both sparkling and dry styles every year, while demi-sec and sweet wines are made only in good to great vintages. Wines from top producers can be very long-lived. Pétillant (semi-sparkling) wines from Vouvray and Montlouis are local specialties. Sauvignon (Blanc) de Touraine, especially from the Cher Valley, can be very good and is often very good value compared to the better-known Pouilly-Fumés and Sancerres. Also of note is the rare Cour-Cheverny made from the little-known Romorantin.

An old wine barrel used as a signpost, Loire Valley

1 Champalou, Cuvée Sw les Fondreaux, Vouvray

ounded in 1985 by idier and Catherine hampalou, this amily estate turns ut an impeccable ange of Vouvrays ear after year. uvée des ondreaux is neir demi-sec uvée, although he level of weetness is ot indicated n the bottle. he honeyed uince fruit is alanced by emony acidity.

Food pairings: Chicken in cream
sauce, pork and prunes
Vintage years: 2006, 2005

2 Domaine Huet, Le Mont Demi-Sec, Vouvray Sw 🛢

Demi-sec or medium-sweet is the traditional style of Vouvray, although Huet makes this style only when the vintage conditions permit. The additional sweetness of the demi-sec allows wines from good vintages to last for decades, becoming more honeyed as they age.

Food pairings: Rich pork dishes
Vintage years: 2006, 2005, 2002

3 Clos Roche Blanche, Touraine Sauvignon

Catherine Roussel and Didier Barouillet of Clos Roche Blanche in the Cher Valley are organic producers of high-quality wines. This wine is usually fairly rich for a Touraine Sauvignon Blanc, thanks to its properly ripened fruit, but it has an attractive minerality. Keeps well for at least five years.

Food pairings: Goat cheese salad
Vintage years: 2007, 2006

4 Domaine Ricard, Le Petiot, Touraine Sauvignon

Based in the Cher Valley, Vincent Ricard is one of the best of the new generation of Touraine producers. Sauvignon Blanc is his specialty, and this is his most popular cuvée. It has an attractive weight and long-lasting grapefruit flavors.

Food pairings: Seafood platter;
goat cheese
Vintage years: 2008

5 Domaine des Huards, Cour-Cheverny 🛢

Cour-Cheverny is an appellation for wines made from the Romoratin grape, a rare variety with the capacity to age 10–20 years. The Gendriers' domaine is run organically. This wine can be lean and austere, although very pure, when young, but develops honeyed flavors with age.

Food pairings: Oysters; cream
cheese
Vintage years: 2005, 2002

1 | **2** |||| **3** | **4** | **5** |

France   185

Rows of vines in New Zealand

growing grapes & making wine

Vines

There are many species of vines but the one that is important for wine is *Vitis vinifera*, which means "wine-producing vine." Within this species there are thousands of individual varieties, and because it naturally mutates over the years, others are constantly being created. Clever scientists also help make new hybrids and crossings to suit particular growing conditions. On the other hand, a great number of varieties are lost each year as regions try to follow fashion and pull up their native, local vines to replace them with well-known, international varieties.

Before the mid 1800s all vines were planted on their own roots, but around the end of the nineteenth century an aphid pest called phylloxera invaded the vineyards of Europe from the East Coast of America and quickly spread, first through France, Spain, and the rest of Europe and then, with a few notable exceptions, around the world. The pest killed the vines, which had a devastating effect on viticulture around the world.

Eventually a solution was found. *Vitis vinifera* vines were grafted onto the native vines of North America, which were a different species—*Vitis riparia*, *Vitis labrusca*, and others. These grafted vines retained their vinifera characteristics but their roots are able to withstand phylloxera. Some vineyard areas such as South Australia, Chile, and a few vineyards within Europe have resisted phylloxera and so still grow vines on their own roots.

Growing the grapes

Location is a very important factor. To thrive and produce grapes for wine, vines need warmth, sunshine, and water in balance. The main grape-growing regions of the world lie in two bands around the world, between 32 and 51° N and between 28 and 44° S, where temperatures are warm enough to ripen the grapes, yet not too hot to retain acidity. Higher-altitude vineyards are cooler, particularly at night, which extends the ripening period and allows for more flavor development, so producers in warm wine regions often plant vineyards on hillsides.

Climate affects the way a vine grows. Average temperatures, day-to-night variation, rain pattern, and sunshine hours all affect the way the grapes develop. Grape varieties are selected to suit the climate and microclimate within a region. A warm sunny slope or a chilly hilltop may require different vines and give totally different results.

Soils vary significantly. There are some vineyards that are as stony as beaches and others as rich and lush as a market garden, but essentially vines prefer well-drained, low-fertility soils so their roots can dig deep. Some varieties do better on specific soil types. Chardonnay thrives on limestone soils, while Riesling is at its most intense when grown on slate. Grape growers work hard to match the right grape variety to the soil they have.

Age is another variable as vines can live more than 100 years, but their most productive years are between 5 and 25 years. After that the yield steadily declines, but in many cases the quality increases. Grape growers have to balance quality and quantity in their vineyard. "Old vine" wines, usually from vines older than 35 years, signify concentration of flavor.

Pruning and yield must be carefully monitored. If allowed to run wild, vines will produce lots of foliage and little fruit. They must be pruned and trained to produce a viable crop, but in general the more grapes they produce, the lower the quality. Once again, the grape grower has to balance quantity and quality. Many growers cut off and throw away part of the crop before it is ripe to help raise the quality of the remaining bunches. This is known as a "green harvest."

Most vineyards around the world have adopted "sustainable viticulture" standards, which means they use minimal sprays on the vines to treat pests and diseases. One step further is organic, which does not permit any chemical sprays or fertilizers to be used on the vines. Only certain natural products are allowed.

Biodynamic viticulture takes a more holistic view of viticulture and takes account of the movement of the moon, the energy of the earth, and the need for certain composts to help the vines grow stronger.

From grapes to wine

The principle of winemaking is simple—grapes contain a sweet juice, which is fermented by yeast into alcohol.

Dry white wine

Sorting involves picking out unripe grapes, leaves, and stems.

Crushing and destemming allows the juice to run out from the grapes—but not so much that the seeds are broken—and removes the stems.

Pressing is a difficult process—the gentler the method of pressing the grapes, the higher the quality of the finished wine.

Yeast can be natural or a commercial strain can be added. Natural yeast may result in a more complex wine, but most wineries use commercial yeasts as they are very reliable.

Fermentation temperature can have a huge effect on the flavors that develop during fermentation. Heat is generated during fermentation, and it is vital to keep it under control when making white wine; fermentation temperatures are usually kept between 59°F and 68°F. In many cases, cooling coils within the tank are used to achieve this.

Lees contact ensures that wines can develop a richer texture and more complex flavors.

Malolactic fermentation transforms harsh malic acid to gentler lactic acid. Although most red wines undergo malolactic fermentation, it is used only for some whites, as crisp acidity is often a desirable quality.

Grapes are crushed gently, to allow the juice to run out. This antique wine press is on display at the Joseph Drouhin Estate in Burgundy

Aging in wooden casks is reserved for some whites with richer, weightier styles. Oak, which has a natural affinity with wine, allows a slow interchange of oxygen between the air and the wine, broadening the texture of the wine and adding its own flavor. French, American, and Eastern European oak is used; each imparts a different character to the finished wine. Casks come in a variety of sizes; the usual barrique is 225 liters (around 50 gallons), but larger casks have a more gentle effect on the wine.

Oak chips and staves are a good alternative to expensive oak barrels. They don't have the same oxygen transfer effect, but they do add texture and flavor to a wine. They have been permitted in many winemaking countries for years, but only recently have they been allowed in Europe for lower-grade wines.

Sweet white wines
In many cases, sweet white wines are made in the same way as dry white wines. It is what happens to the grapes before harvest that makes all the difference. Some sweet wines are made from late-harvested grapes. The grapes are left to ripen on the vine for longer than usual, developing higher levels of sugar as they do so. (Examples are VDN wines from Alsace, and Auslese wines from Germany.)

In other cases, the grapes are raisined before they are pressed, concentrating the sugars. There are two main methods of doing so. The stalks that attach the bunches of grapes can be partially cut and the grapes raisined while still on the vine (a technique known in France as *passerillage*). Sweet wines from Jurançon are made this way. Alternatively, the harvested grapes can be dried in a winery loft. In this instance, the bunches are either hung vertically from hooks or laid out on dry, neutral material. (Recioto di Soave from the Veneto is made with this method.)

Other sweet wines are made by exposing the bunches of ripe grapes to infection by a fungus known as *Botrytis cinerea*, also referred to as noble rot. This concentrates the sugars in the grapes while also imparting a distinctive flavor to the finished wine. (Examples are Sauternes from Bordeaux, and the sweet Chenin Blancs of the Loire.)

Ice wines (or *Eisweine*, as they are known in Germany) are made by leaving the grapes on the vine until temperatures plummet to 18°F or below. The grapes freeze on the vine and, when they are pressed, the ice crystals are left in the press and only the sweet juice, which has a lower freezing point than water, runs out. Mainly made in Canada and Germany, ice wines are usually made from Vidal and Riesling. Due to small yields and the labor-intensive processes involved, these wines are expensive, but they can be exquisite and well worth seeking out.

Vines for *Eiswein*, Rheingau, Germany

Fortified wines

The winemaking for fortified wines (which include sherries and Ports) follows the same processes as those for "normal" white wines until the required amount of residual sugar remains (in the case of fino or manzanilla sherries, they are fermented dry, but most fortified wines have some sugar left in them). At that point, grape spirit is added to the wine, which stops fermentation and raises the alcohol level to the required degree, which ranges from 15 percent in dry sherries to 20 percent in port. Some fortified wines are then aged in a solera.

Rosé wines

Other than some very basic still wines, and (at the opposite end of the spectrum) rosé Champagnes, few rosés are made by blending red and white wines together. Most rosé is made by running off some of the juice from red grapes after a short period of maceration. The remaining red grape juice will usually go on to be fermented as a red wine, while the lightly colored juice that has been bled off is made into rosé. Wines made using this technique are often known as *rosé de saignée*.

Champagne

Champagne begins life as a still white wine. It is only when the fermentation is complete that additional processes turn the still wine into one with bubbles.

Méthode traditionelle

This method, also known as *méthode champenoise*, is used to make a number of other sparkling wines, including many of France's crémants, cavas, and New World sparkling wines. Second fermentation combines a liquid known as *liqueur de tirage* into the blended wine. A mixture of wine, sugar, and yeast, it sparks off a second fermentation in the bottle.

The yeasts metabolize the sugar, turning it into alcohol and carbon dioxide before dying back to leave a deposit on the side of the bottle.

Maturation causes the dead yeast cells to break down and the enzymes interact with the wine in a process called autolysis, adding yeasty flavors to the wine. NV (non-vintage) Champagnes spend at least 15 months aging in the bottle, while vintage Champagnes spend at least three years in the bottle.

Disgorgement helps to remove the sediment; the bottles are gradually moved from a horizontal position to a near-horizontal one. Traditionally this was done by hand, a process known as riddling, but now the process is largely mechanized. Once the deposit has slipped down into the neck of the bottle, the neck is briefly frozen and the cap removed. The plug of ice, which contains the sediment, is expelled from the bottle at high velocity.

Dosage means that the bottle is topped off with a mixture known as *liqueur d'expedition*—a mixture of wine and sugar—to refill the small amount of wine that is lost during disgorgement. The amount of sugar used depends on the style of wine and the Champagne house's own recipe.

The Charmat method

In some instances, the yeasty character of Champagne is considered undesirable, particularly when making fresh, fruity sparkling wines, such as Germany's Sekt and Italy's Prosecco. The second fermentation of such wines takes place in a sealed tank. The sediment is removed by filtration under pressure before the wine is bottled. One key downside of using the Charmat process is that the bubbles do not last as long as those derived from bottle fermentation.

leading grape varieties

Albariño/Alvarinho is the star of white Spanish grape varieties. Albariño produces perfumed, peachy wines with lively acidity. It is closely associated with the coastal Rías Baixas region, where it is the most widely planted grape. Wines made from Albariño are rarely matured in oak and are generally enjoyed young. In northern Portugal the variety is known as Alvarinho.

Chardonnay's success is due to its ability to adapt to climates and soils throughout the world and the versatility that it offers the winemaker as a blending component. It also has a strong affinity with oak.

Some of the finest styles of Chardonnay, including crisp, minerally Chablis wines, can be found in Burgundy, the grape's original home. But each country or winemaker offers a different take on the grape—Californian styles can be exotic, buttery, and full-bodied while those of Chile or New Zealand are more restrained with delicate citrus flavors. Chardonnay also plays a major role in the Champagne blend and good-quality traditional method sparkling wines elsewhere.

Chenin Blanc is a particularly versatile grape, and a highly respected variety in the Loire Valley. One of its attributes is good acidity, which gives both dry and honeyed sweet wines made from the variety the ability to last and develop. It can be found in other countries, notably South Africa, where it is also known as Steen. Some of the best South African whites are produced from old-vine Chenin Blanc.

Gewürztraminer is one of the wine world's most exotic and aromatic grapes. Often characterized by delicate lychee fruit, Gewürztraminer is widely grown in Alsace in eastern France, where particularly fine late-harvest wines are made from the variety. It can also be found in Germany, northern Italy, Eastern Europe, and many parts of the New World, albeit in small quantities. Gewürztraminer is not a fan of oak.

Grüner Veltliner is Austria's signature grape, and produces distinctive, full-bodied wines with steely freshness and an occasional hint of pepper. The grape is generally used to make dry, unoaked, food-friendly wines.

Marsanne is a fashionable French variety, hailing from the northern Rhône Valley. Usually part of a blend, Marsanne contributes structure, generous alcohol, and rich fruit character. It adapts well in Australia's Goulbourn Valley and California's Central Coast region.

Muscadelle is native to Bordeaux, and specifically Entre-Deux-Mers. Muscadelle has a lesser but still valuable role alongside Sémillon and Sauvignon in both dry and sweet wines. The variety contributes elegance and an aromatic quality.

Muscat varieties appear in many different guises and under many names. Muscat grapes are responsible for some of the finest sweet wines. They are the only variety that actually smells of fresh grapes. Depending on winemaking and age, Muscat wines range from pale, white grapey young wines to much darker, rich styles. There are four main Muscat varieties. The most superior, Muscat Blanc à Petits Grains, is responsible for famous sweet wines such as Beaumes-de-Venise. Its many other synonyms include Muscat of Frontignan, Muscat d'Alsace, Moscato d'Asti, Moscato di Canelli, and Moscatel de Grano Menudo. Other widely found varieties are Muscat of Alexandria, Muscat Hamburg, and Muscat Ottonel.

Pinot Blanc is a fairly neutral but elegant grape, widely planted in Alsace where it is used for both still and sparkling wines. In Italy it is known as Pinot Bianco, and in Austria as Weissburgunder. The variety can also be found in Oregon and California.

Pinot Grigio/Pinot Gris has become one of the most popular grapes. This pink-skinned grape, usually hailing from Italy, can offer little character. However, finer examples of the grape with far more aromatic character and richer styles are produced from lower yields and quality-oriented producers in the Veneto, Friuli, and the Alto Adige.

In France, where it is known as Pinot Gris, its heartland is Alsace, where the grape makes both dry and fine late-harvest wines. It is even more common in Germany, as Grauburgunder or Ruländer (to describe sweet wines), and it also features in Central Europe. In the New World, it has adapted well in New Zealand, Australia, and the state of Oregon in the U.S.

Riesling (pictured left) is the star German grape, and is widely acknowledged as one of the wine world's most interesting characters. It ripens early and prefers cooler climates; its excellent natural acidity makes it a good candidate for cellaring. In Germany, huge importance is given to the location of the vineyard to determine the character of a Riesling wine rather than any winemaking intervention. The time of harvest and residual sugar determine the style, which can range from dry, crisp wines with attractive limey fruit to rich, honeyed, sweet wines.

Riesling has been successfully adopted in Australia—in the cooler Clare and Eden Valleys, Western Australia, and Tasmania—as well as in New Zealand. Good Rieslings can also be found in Oregon and Washington in the U.S., and the Riesling ice wines of Canada are particularly impressive. Rhine Riesling should not be confused with more ordinary grapes with a similar name such as Cape Riesling, Riesling Italico, and Welschriesling.

Roussanne hails from the northern Rhône, and is often paired with Marsanne, its regional sibling. It can also be found in southern France, Savoie (as Bergeron), and California. The best wines made from the variety are elegant and long-lasting.

Sauvignon Blanc (pictured right) is one of the most expressive grape varieties. It is highly aromatic and given little contact with oak beyond a little barrel fermentation in some regions. Sauvignon Blanc wines take on a different guise according to country and region. The fresh, lively Sauvignons of the Loire Valley are quite different from their more restrained but perhaps more food-friendly cousins of Bordeaux.

New Zealand is particularly well-known for assertive examples of Sauvignon Blanc, which can offer a myriad of flavors from gooseberry, asparagus, and grass to riper tropical fruit-flavored wines. Wine producers in Chile, South Africa, and even Argentina also offer good Sauvignons from cooler climate areas. New World producers increasingly favor screwcap closures for Sauvignon Blanc wines to preserve their aromas and freshness.

Sémillon (Semillon outside France) is almost exclusively associated with Bordeaux in France. Most significantly it is the grape of Sauternes, the famous sweet wine made from shrivelled noble rot grapes—Sémillon's thin skin makes it susceptible to the humid atmosphere of Sauternes and Barsac and ideal for the wine style. Sémillon is blended with Sauvignon Blanc and occasionally Muscadelle to make Bordeaux's dry white wines, adding structure and texture to blends. Although the variety can be found quite widely beyond France, Australia is unquestionably Semillon's most successful country of adoption. In the Hunter Valley, dry Semillons, generally full-bodied in style, can develop an enticing rich lime fruit character and are capable of aging impressively. Richer styles of Semillon can also be found in the hotter Barossa Valley.

Viognier is the most popular grape from the northern Rhône and the highly regarded grape of Condrieu. Viognier can also be found in southern France, California, South Africa, and Australia. It performs at its best in warm climates, producing full-bodied wines easily recognized by their intense perfume and apricot fruit.

regional white varieties

Arneis is native to Italy's Piedmont in the northwest and is used to make the dry, herbaceous grape of Roero.

Assyrtiko is widely acknowledged as Greece's finest white grape. Assyrtiko makes both dry white wines and fine amber-colored dessert wines.

Bacchus is an early ripening variety that makes wines similar in style to Sauvignon Blanc in Germany and England.

Fernão Pires is one of many Portuguese grapes of character. Fernão Pires is grown throughout the country and particularly in Ribatejo and Bairrada, where it is known as Maria Gomes.

Fiano is an ancient grape of southern Campania in Italy, where it gives its name to Fiano di Avellino wines. It is also widely planted in Sicily.

Friulano is widely planted in the Italian region of Friuli where it makes a crisp, nutty wine. The variety is also known as Sauvignonasse.

Furmint (pictured, right) is a Hungarian grape and the main grape used in the sweet Tokaji wines, as it is susceptible to noble rot. Often paired with the more aromatic Hárselvelú grape.

Garganega is the Soave grape—the best wines are made from low-yielding vines situated on slopes.

Greco is one of Italy's many interesting ancient varieties and also a native of Campania. It gives its name to Greco di Tufo wines.

Grenache Blanc is a Mediterranean variety and the white partner of Grenache Noir/Garnacha Tinta. Wines made from the variety are generally for early drinking. Often paired with other southern French varieties such as Grenache Gris.

Petit Manseng and Gros Manseng are native to southwest France. Petit Manseng, featuring smaller berries and thicker skins, is the superior of the two and used for sweet wines including Pacherenc du Vic-Bilh. Gros Manseng is used for drier Juraçon wines.

Malvasia is a fragrant grape native to the Mediterranean and southern Europe. It is found in Friuli as Malvasia Istriana and in neighboring Slovenia as well as Rioja where it partners with Viura. The variety is also found in Portugal and Madeira.

Melon de Bourgogne is a fairly neutral grape used to make crisp, fresh Muscadet wines in the Loire. More sophisticated wines are made from the variety by sur lie aging.

Palomino Fino is the main sherry grape of southern Spain. Palomino Fino is a neutral grape that transforms into something far more interesting and a myriad of styles when it comes into contact with oak.

Pedro Ximénez is an intriguing grape found mostly in the hot, dry region of Montilla. It is used to make sweet, molasses-like wines.

Rolle/Vermentino is an aromatic Mediterranean variety. The name of Rolle is generally used in southern France, and Vermentino in Sardinia and western Italy. It makes lively, fresh wines.

Torrontés is a Muscat-like variety grown in most regions of Argentina. A grape of the same name can also be found in Galicia.

Verdejo is one of Spain's more interesting white grapes, and is found in Rueda in western Spain. It is often blended with Sauvignon Blanc (pictured left).

Verdicchio hails from the Marche region of Italy, where it makes wines with good structure and a hint of spice.

Viura is also known as Macabeo, and is a fairly neutral wine used for still wines in Rioja. It responds well to oak.

Rosé wines

Many red grapes are suitable for making rosé wines; indeed some of the best rosé wines are blended from several varieties, combining the attributes of each grape.

In southern France, Grenache is a popular traditional choice, as this variety offers both generous fruit character and acidity. The same grape, known locally as Garnacha, makes some of the best Spanish rosés in Navarra, while Tempranillo is generally the grape of choice for Rioja's rosés. Syrah makes rosés with plenty of spicy fruit character, especially in the New World; other popular choices for rosés with plenty of juicy red fruit character are Cabernet Sauvignon and Merlot.

Regional grapes for rosé wines include Malbec in Argentina, Pinotage in South Africa, and Zinfandel (pictured right) in California. The well-known Rosé d'Anjou wines of the Loire are made from the Grolleau grape.

Champagne and sparkling wines

Champagne producers select from three grapes to make their various wine styles: Chardonnay, Pinot Noir, and Pinot Meunier. Chardonnay, the only white variety of the trio, contributes finesse; Pinot Noir gives structure and depth of fruit; and Pinot Meunier offers richness.

Chardonnay and Pinot Noir are generally used by quality-oriented New World producers to make traditional method sparkling wines—especially in California, Australia, New Zealand, and South Africa. Many English sparkling wine producers use all three grapes.

In Spain, cava sparkling wines are made mainly from three local white grapes: Parellada, Macabeo, and Xarel-lo. Chardonnay is occasionally used and, for rosé cavas, Pinot Noir.

The most popular Italian sparkling wine is Prosecco. It is made from the grape of the same name and comes from the Veneto region in the northeast of the country.

Asking the wine seller is a good start when you are faced with rows of daunting bottles

selecting wine

One of the easiest ways to buy a bottle of wine for tonight's supper or next week's family dinner is to buy the wine you enjoyed last week. There's no risk, you know you liked it, and it will probably go reasonably well with whatever is on the menu. But just before you reach for that same bottle, think again. If you are in a big supermarket, you probably have around 800 wines in front of you. That's 800 different combinations of flavor, region, and grape variety. Even if you drink a bottle of wine every night, and you have an endless supply of money, it would take over two years to try them all. So why waste one of those occasions by buying the same wine you drank last week?

Everyone has their favorites and we should rejoice in coming back to familiar flavors, but one of the great pleasures of buying and tasting wine is that each one is different. It has come from a different place, it has been made in a different way, and its flavors are resolutely different.

But how should you go about selecting a different wine? You could take note of the grape variety of the bottle that you enjoyed. If it was a Chardonnay from California, then why not try the same grape from Chile, or Australia, or perhaps France? Try following the flavors of a grape around the world. Or take an in-depth look at the wines from one country. Start in Italy and try wines from Soave, Friuli, Tuscany, Campania, and Sicily.

Shopping

One of the best things about buying from a supermarket is that there is no one to pressure you into buying something too expensive. It is easy to find something within your budget and to escape through the checkout without anyone raising an eyebrow. But in general there is no one to ask about wine. If you read the back label, you will learn a little, but it is not the same as finding out about how it tastes.

A dedicated wine store is completely different. Here the people will probably have a lot of experience in wine and they are keen to sell you something good. They probably will have tasted most of the wines in the store, and their job is not to sell you the most expensive one. They want to sell you the wine that is right for you, and they hope you will come back next week so they can do it all over again. There will probably be wines available to taste, so you can see if you like it. These tasting wines will not be the most expensive wine, but they will probably not be the cheapest either, so you can start to get a feel for what is in their range.

Wine tastings

Regular wine tastings might be held at that dedicated wine store. For a small sum, you can taste dozens of wines so you can really grow to appreciate the flavors from around the world. Get on their mailing list so you can also find out about visiting winemakers and attending gourmet dinners and other events that will open up the world of wine to you. One of the best ways to learn about wine is to get together with a group of friends, form a club, and meet regularly to share bottles. If you can do this in your own neighborhood, preferably within walking distance, you will not only be able to taste the wines, but also to drink and enjoy them.

The tasting room with a view of the vineyard at Domaine Chandon, Australia

The best clubs are made up of no more than 16 members. That is because you will get around 16 tasting samples from each bottle, and for most people this is enough people to have in their home. One person should be appointed to arrange the next tasting. His or her job is to read up about a region and then select some wines to show the diversity within that region. The wines are tasted seriously, and then probably enjoyed over a supper.

It sounds boring, but by the time you get home you will have forgotten which of those wines you liked best. I have met many people in front of wine shelves in stores as they puzzle over the labels — did the wine they liked have a green label or was it yellow? Was it Sauvignon Blanc or Sémillon? If you haven't written it down, you will forget. We all do. Start a notebook and write down what you tasted and whether you liked it.

Selecting wine in a restaurant

The same rules apply in restaurants as they do in stores. The easy way is always to choose the same wine, to stay in the comfort zone of price and familiarity, but you may do better if you ask the wine waiter for advice. He knows the menu and what will really complement the food. He might also be able to give you suggestions to cope with a table where some people are eating fish and the others venison. A wine waiter or sommelier will always try to talk up sales, but if you give him a price limit he should come up with three suggestions—low, middle, and high price.

If there is nobody to ask, then it is worth looking at lesser-known regions for the real bargains. The wine list will probably make bigger profits on the well-known, reliable wines, but if you try some of the less-known wines, you may get more flavor for your money.

If two of you have chosen wildly different dishes, there may not be a compromise wine. In this case you could select wine by the glass, so long as the restaurant has a regular turnover or one of those clever inert gas systems that keeps opened bottles fresh.

Cork or screwcap?

A few years ago all wine bottles were sealed with a cork, apart from the real cheap ones with a screwcap. Then brightly colored plastic stoppers arrived, followed by a whole array of different stoppers, agglomerates, specially treated agglomerates, and upmarket screwcaps, which often go by the brand name of Stelvin. Why the change? Toward the end of the twentieth century, the demand for cork had grown so high that the whole industry was under strain. When that happened, standards dropped and the incidence of "cork taint" grew to alarming proportions. At one point it was reckoned that around one bottle in every case of 12 was affected by a musty, corky taste that made the wine undrinkable. That was the trigger for alternatives to move into the market.

Now the cork industry has improved its standards and the incidence of cork taint has subsided, but we still have the array of closures, in particular the screwcap, which has shown itself to be particularly good for fresh-tasting white wines, rosés, and lighter styles of reds that don't need aging.

Will it keep?

One of the first questions many people ask about wine is whether it will keep. There seems to be a built-in assumption that wine will improve if you lay it down and leave it for a couple of years. For the vast majority of wine on the shelves, this is wrong. Most wine is made to be drinkable when you buy it. Its fresh fruity flavors are there, just waiting for you to enjoy. Some wines, particularly reds, do need time to develop and age, but, with a few exceptions, this is seldom true of whites. The best way to find out is to ask the person you buy it from. Otherwise use this rule—wines costing less than $20 are unlikely to improve much with age, although they won't come to any harm if you keep them for a year or so, whereas wines costing over $20 may develop more interesting flavors with age.

As an added guide, it's worth bearing the following in mind:

Non-vintage Champagne and New World sparkling wines can often repay a few months' aging in bottle, but aren't worth keeping for more than a year or two.

Vintage Champagne can be aged for many years.

Cavas, Sekts, and Proseccos should be enjoyed young.

Top-quality Chardonnay from a good vintage can age and develop for a decade or more, especially if it comes from a cool climate.

Wines with high levels of acidity, particularly Rieslings and Chenin Blancs, age well. One notable exception is Sauvignon Blanc, which is best enjoyed young.

Good-quality dessert wines will usually age well.

Rosé wines are best enjoyed within a year of the vintage date.

Whatever its age, old wine is unlikely to go off. It certainly will not harm you, but it may have lost some of the fruit character that the winemaker intended to be there. On the other hand, it may have evolved into a gloriously complex wine. Just pull the cork and try it. One of the best ways to find out how a wine ages is to buy a dozen bottles. Keep them in a safe place and from time to time open one of the bottles to enjoy with supper. Over the months and years you will get to know the flavors and how they evolve. Write down your thoughts and keep your notes safe. Before you have finished that case of wine, buy another, the same or something different. Pretty soon you have a cellar, enjoying the changing flavors of wine as they age.

Barrel cellar, Jarnac, France

storing and serving wine

The best place to keep your wine is in a wine cellar, at a constant temperature between 40°F and 50°F, in the dark with no vibration. The bottles should be horizontal or angled so that the cork (if there is one) is kept moist. But since most of us do not have cellars, then the best alternative is a north-facing room, a cupboard away from direct heat, or even a corner in an insulated garage. Keep a thermometer near your wine, preferably one of those maximum and minimum ones that will tell you whether your chosen place varies a lot in temperature. If it does, then try to insulate around the rack, to keep temperature fluctuations as little as possible. A wine rack is ideal and can be used for bottles with all kinds of stoppers, but if the bottle has a screwcap there is no need to keep it horizontal.

Glasses

Good wine should taste the same no matter whether it arrives in a plastic cup or a fine glass—but it does not. After being in the bottle for several months or years, wine needs space and air to open up in the glass, so it is worthwhile investing in a good set of glasses. They should be made of clear glass, tulip-shaped, wider at the bowl than at the rim, and with stems, so you can hold the glass without touching the bowl of the glass. Holding the bowl warms up the wine, and prevents you from seeing the glorious deep, rich colors in the wine. Fill the glass no more than half-full to allow the wine room to breathe and space for you to swirl it around to release the aromas.

In a perfect world, glasses should be washed by hand and rinsed in clear water before being polished dry with a clean linen cloth. In reality dishwashers are fine, but rinse-aid residue on the glass can reduce the bubbles in sparkling wines.

Store glasses upright. Inverting them traps a pocket of air which could taint the wine

Serving temperatures

The general rule for serving wine is that white wines should be chilled and red wines should be served at room temperature, but this is far too general. For a start, room temperature doesn't mean the temperature of your kitchen when you have been cooking all day, nor does it mean the living room, close to a radiator or a roaring fire.

The ideal serving temperature for white wines will depend on the style of the wine in question. Generally speaking, if you serve a wine too cool, the aromatic compounds that provide its appeal will not be able to evaporate, so you will lose the pleasure of its bouquet. However, wines served too warm can appear soupy and alcoholic.

As a broad rule of thumb, light and crisp styles of white, such as Riesling, Muscadet, and Sauvignon Blanc, as well as sparkling wines of all kinds and Fino and Manzanilla sherries, should be served between 43°F and 47°F. Fuller styles of white wine, such as rich, oaky Chardonnay or Viognier, can be served a bit warmer—somewhere between 48°F and 52°F is about right. This is also the ideal temperature range for most sweet white wines and Amontillado and Oloroso sherries. Rosés should be served at a temperature ranging between 50°F and 54°F.

If you find you've served your wine at the wrong temperature, the problem is easy to fix. Keep a bottle sleeve in the freezer, ready to cool a bottle down, or stick the bottle in a bucket or other container with a mixture of ice and cold water. If, on the other hand, the wine is a bit cold, cup the bowl of the glass in your hand to warm it up.

Decanters

Even wine professionals debate the merits of decanting white wines. Broadly speaking, few white wines benefit from being decanted before serving. The possible exceptions are young examples of richer whites, such as those from Meursault or Puligny Montrachet, Condrieus, and some of the bigger wines from southern France, which may benefit from a bit of aeration. However, not even purists would claim this is a vital step.

Wine served too cold can easily be warmed up in your hand before drinking

The most effective way to taste wine uses all the senses

how to taste

This must surely be the easiest part of wine drinking. Well, it is, but like all things, the more you put into it, the more you get out. For a start, the overall taste of a wine is a complex combination of taste and smell. The nose is equally, if not more, important to the overall appreciation of flavor as the tongue. The palate itself can distinguish only between sweetness, acidity, bitterness, salt, and a savoriness known as umami. All the rest of the flavors—the hints of peaches, white flowers, lemon zest, and spice—come from the olfactory area of the nose, which picks up these signals from molecules swept up into the nasal cavity. If you swirl the wine around in the glass and then sniff, you will find these aromas. When the wine is in the mouth, if you "chew" it or slurp in some air—professional wine tasters slurp quite dreadfully—these molecules will register as flavors in your brain.

Apart from the flavor components, the most vital aspects of a white wine to notice are its levels of acidity and sugar. Acidity forms the backbone of a white wine; without sufficient levels, a wine will appear flabby and unfocused. While many, if not most, white wines are dry, others have discernible levels of sugar that can range from off-dry to lusciously sweet, depending on the style. Whatever the level of sweetness, it is vital that it is balanced by acidity, otherwise the wine will come across as cloying.

Just remember how you used to drink something horrid as a child. You held your nose. If you don't use your nose in wine tasting, you are missing most of the fun. You can also detect alcohol in the mouth, as warmth on the back of the palate.

Tasting words

At your first wine tasting, you will probably come across a person who describes a wine like this, "Crisp and floral with citrussy freshness and hints of peach and a hot finish," and all you can taste is—well, wine. Have you got it wrong? Are your tastebuds defective? No and no.

Wine tasting takes practice and so does its vocabulary. Imagine trying to explain the taste of a lamb chop to someone who has never tasted one. It is difficult. The best way to build your own vocabulary is to enjoy life with your nose open. Smell the gooseberries straight from the garden, still warm with sunshine, and then think of Sauvignon Blanc. Don't just eat that ripe apricot, get your nose in there and smell it. Then think of Viognier. Next time you make bread, sniff the yeasty aromas as it rises. Think about that when you next pour yourself a glass of Champagne. Or cut open a couple of limes and a lemon and then open a bottle of Australian Riesling. All these experiences will help you build up your own vocabulary. And if you think peaches when the next guy thinks melons, you are both right. Writing tasting notes is just finding a peg to hang a flavor on. Whatever notes you take, they are your notes, no one else's.

Rosé wine is seldom a blend of red and white wines

Champagne with smoked salmon–wrapped bread sticks and a poached egg

food and wine

Good with food. These three words appear on more wine labels than you can count. But what kind of food?

As with all things in life there are no absolute rules, but there are certain affinities between food and wine that will help you find the best combinations.

Think about weight—not the amount of food on the plate but the weight and texture of the food in your mouth. Light foods such as salads and plain broiled fish need light wines to accompany them, and as the food choices become heavier —roast chicken, fish dishes with sauce—you need wines with more weight and texture to balance them. Acidity is important, too; tomato-rich dishes need a wine with some acidity to balance them. And think about sugar levels. Wines that are off-dry are great complements to spiced Asian dishes, and don't even think about matching a dry wine to dessert—a good rule of thumb is to ensure that the wine is at least as sweet as the dessert, otherwise it will appear dry and harsh.

at-a-glance food pairings

Food	Sauce or flavoring	Wine suggestion
Asparagus	Vinaigrette or a squeeze of lemon	Sauvignon Blanc or Sémillon-Sauvignon blends
Artichokes	Vinaigrette	Fino or Manzanilla sherry
Green salads		Crisp, dry whites such as Sauvignon Blanc, Riesling
Seafood salads		Verdelho, Albariño, Chablis
Shrimp	A squeeze of lemon or lime, chile sauce	Sauvignon Blanc, Australian Riesling
Shrimp	Tomato and garlic sauce	White blends from Southern France, Sicilian whites & rosés
Seafood platter		Chablis, Muscadet, Picpoul de Pinet
Scallops	Thai flavors, such as lime and lemongrass	New World Riesling, New Zealand Sauvignon Blanc
Scallops	Cream or butter sauces	Burgundies or other oaked Chardonnays, Viognier
Lobster		Burgundy, Californian Chardonnay, Champagne, Viognier
Bouillabaisse or seafood stews		Southern French whites, Albariño, Rosé
Sashimi		Riesling, young Chenin, Assyrtiko
Sushi		Marsanne, Roussanne, Albariño, Sicilian whites
Southern Indian seafood curries		Aromatic whites from Alsace
Thai stir-fries and salads		Riesling, Sauvignon Blanc
Chinese stir-fries		Pinot Gris, Grüner Veltliner
Light white fish, such as sole	Lemon, butter, and herbs	Chablis, Sauvignon-Sémillon blends
Sea bass	Aromatic herbs	Albariño, Vermentino
Mackerel, sardines, or other oily fish		Sauvignon Blanc, Picpoul de Pinet, Vinho Verde, Assyrtiko
Turbot		Sauvignon-Sémillon blends from Bordeaux, Burgundy
Salmon	Cold, with mayonnaise	Chardonnay
Salmon	Hollandaise	Top-quality Chardonnay, from either New World or Burgundy
Salmon	Grilled	Rosé

Food	Sauce or flavoring	Wine suggestion
Smoked salmon		Champagne, Pouilly Fumé, Sancerre, Grüner Veltliner
Gravlax		Off-dry Riesling or Chenin Blanc
Tuna		Rosé
Fish pie		Chardonnay
Fried fish with french fries		Sauvignon Blanc, Albarino
Chicken	Roast	Chardonnay, Southern French whites
Chicken	With tomatoes and garlic	Rosé
Goose	Roast, with applesauce	Spätlese Riesling
Pork	Roast	Chardonnay, Sémillon, Grenache Blanc and Gris
Pork	With apricots	Viognier
Pasta	Tomato-based sauce	Pinot Grigio, Verdicchio
Pasta	Pesto	Soave
Pasta	Creamy sauce	Pinot Blanc, Southern Italian whites
Paella		White Rioja (especially modern styles)
Risotto	Seafood or vegetable	Crisp northern Italian white or Soave
Risotto	Shellfish, roast squash	New World Semillon, Verdicchio
Hard cheeses	Cheddar, Parmesan, Manchego	Amontillado or Oloroso sherry
Goat cheeses		Sauvignon Blanc, Bacchus
Sheep's cheeses		Off-dry Riesling from Alsace, Alsatian Pinot Gris
Blue cheeses	Stilton, Roquefort	Sweet wines such as Sauternes or Côteaux du Layon
Strawberries		Moscato d'Asti
Crème brûlée, crème caramel		Sauternes-styles wines, Saussignac
Fruit cake		Rutherglen Muscat, Fortified Muscats, Vin Santo, Tokaji
Fruit tarts		Sauternes-style wines, sweet Rieslings
Biscotti, Cantuccini		Vin Santo

glossary

Acidity	Naturally present in grapes, acidity gives freshness to a wine and helps it age. Too much can make the wine taste sharp.
Aging	Aging a white wine in tank, cask, or bottle allows complexity to develop—this is especially true of white Burgundies, Rieslings, sweet wines, and top Champagnes. Too much aging can cause a wine to lose its fruit flavors.
Barrel/barrique	Barrique is the name for a 225-liter (50-gallon) barrel traditionally used in France. Usually made of French oak, barriques are used in many wineries around the world for aging and sometimes for fermenting wine.
Biodynamic	This is a holistic approach to viticulture and winemaking, taking into account the forces of the moon and the energy of the earth.
Blending	A wine may be made of several different grape varieties, all of which may ripen at different times. Once the wines have been made, they will be blended to create a wine with a more complex flavor.
Botrytis cinerea	A fungus that grows on grapes and dehydrates them, concentrating their sugars. A vital part of the process used to create some of the world's best sweet wines, including Sauternes, and Germany's TBA Rieslings. Also known as noble rot.
Canopy	The growth of the leaves, stems, and fruit above ground.
Cépage	French for grape variety.
Cru	French for a single vineyard, often used to signify specific quality—for example, Burgundy has Premier and Grand Cru vineyards as well as those used to grow grapes that go into Village or generic Bourgogne wines.
Cuvée	A type, blend, or batch of wine. Often used to denote a particular wine within a range made by a producer, such as Joe Bloggs' Chardonnay cuvée.
Fermentation	A process whereby yeast transforms grape sugars into alcohol.
Hybrid	A vine created by crossing the normal wine-producing vine, *Vitis vinifera*, with another vine species. This is usually done to create a combination of desirable characteristics in the resulting plant.
Ice wine	Made from grapes allowed to freeze on the vines, then picked and the juice squeezed out under pressure and fermented. Generally very sweet.
Lees	The sediment that settles at the bottom of the fermentation vessel. It is made up of dead yeast cells, pulp, skin fragments, and insoluble tartrates.

Malolactic fermentation	A secondary fermentation (after the alcoholic fermentation), which transforms harsh malic acid to softer lactic acids. Almost all red wines and some whites go through this process.
Microclimate	The immediate area around a vine that has an effect on the way it grows.
Négociant	French term for a wine merchant or trader who buys wine and grapes, blends it, and ships under his own label. Not a producer.
Oak	The most common wood used for wine casks. Oak can come from various countries, with French, American, and Eastern European oak most commonly used. Each imparts its own distinct character to a wine.
Organic	Organic viticulture restricts the use of chemical pesticides and fertilizers, although treatments with some naturally occurring products such as sulfur and copper are permitted. Actual regulations vary across the world but are generally of a good standard.
Residual sugar	The amount of sugar left in a wine after fermentation is completed (or, in the case of fortified wines, stopped by the addition of grape spirit).
Solera	A system designed to smooth out the differences between vintage years by blending wines from consecutive vintages with each other in a set ratio. For example, if 20 percent of a barrel containing five-year-old wine is bottled, the barrel is topped off with 20 percent of the contents of the four-year-old barrel, which is topped off in turn by 20 percent of the contents of the three-year-old barrel, and so on until the current vintage is reached. Soleras can be active for decades.
Sulfur	A naturally occurring element that acts as a natural disinfectant, preventing microbial spoilage. Commonly used in the wine and food industries.
Terroir	A French term used around the world to describe the interaction between the soil, location, and climate of a vineyard. It is the terroir that gives a wine its regional identity.
Vintage	The actual year of production. It has no particular quality connotations.
Yeast	The yeast *Saccharomyces cerevisiae* is naturally found on grape skins in vineyards around the world and is used to ferment sugars into alcohol. Specific strains of this yeast may be cultured on an industrial scale and then used in wine fermentation to generate specific flavors.
Yield	The amount of fruit a vine can produce. In broad terms, if yield is restricted, flavors are more concentrated. An optimum crop is one that is commercially viable yet produces flavorful grapes.

North America

Being a wine producer in North America has often required steely determination and tenacity; from the time the first colonists arrived, there have been many hurdles to overcome.

At the outset appropriate vine material had to be established to produce a more palatable wine. Then problems of vineyard disease had to be tackled—indeed some enemies of the vine such as Pierce's disease have a nasty habit of recurring to this day. Another setback, perhaps the worst of all, was Prohibition, which brought wine producers to their knees from 1918 to 1933.

Given this backdrop, it's remarkable that wine production is such an important and vibrant industry across the continent today. In terms of ranking, the U.S. is the largest producer of wine after France, Italy, and Spain. The lion's share of quality wine is accounted for by California, home to famous appellations such as Napa Valley. Farther north, the states of Oregon and Washington have raised their game in recent years, using grapes well adapted to their regions, including Pinot Gris. Meanwhile, over the border in British Columbia and Ontario, Canada's winemakers now offer impressive cooler climate wines including highly prized ice wines.

Stretching from the eastern coast to Niagara Falls, New York State is busy reinventing itself as a serious contender in the wine world, though its wines have yet to leave America's shores in significant quantities. If the impressive Rieslings of the Finger Lakes are an indication of progress, this wine region is heading in the right direction.

1. Mendocino & Lake County
2. Sonoma
3. Napa
4. Santa Cruz, Monterey & Central Coast regions
5. Central Valley

CALIFORNIA

The Pacific Ocean and it's large bays temper the climate in most Californian wine regions, providing cool winds and fogs that balance the heat and sunshine. Although drought can be a hazard, most regions receive 24–45 inches of rain annually.

California

California's winemaking history dates back to the late 1700s, when Spanish missionaries introduced vines from Mexico. There are currently around 100 AVA (American Viticultural Areas) stretching along the Pacific Coast north and south of San Francisco and inland to the Central Valley. This gives the Golden State the lion's share of America's wine production as well as some of the most scenic vineyard country in the world.

The Pacific Ocean is the state's most significant geographical aspect for wine production. Its cool waters cause a cooling blanket of fog that moderates temperatures for vineyards, especially those with a coastal location.

California's wine producers have fully recovered from their 1990s battle with phylloxera, the deadly vine louse, which destroyed many acres of vineyard. Vineyard owners turned their misfortune into an opportunity by matching grape varieties to sites more effectively as they replanted. As a result, wine lovers have been rewarded with better quality and a greater choice of wines from the state.

Mendocino County

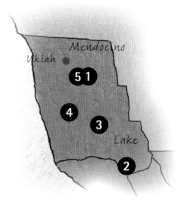

Rugged and mountainous Mendocino is situated at the northernmost point of California's wine regions. Its focal point is Anderson Valley and the Navarro River, which is lined by wineries on each side. The particularly cool growing season here makes it an ideal location for varieties such as Chardonnay and Pinot Noir, staples for fine sparkling wines. The Italian immigrants who settled here many years ago found that Zinfandel, a favorite choice for rosés, is also well suited to the slopes of the Anderson Valley as well as the warmer Lake County vineyards to the east.

Navarro Vineyards—close to the Navarro River, the climate is perfect for winegrowing

1 Parducci, Sauvignon Blanc

Paul Dolan heads up winemaking for Parducci, a producer with a strong commitment to sustainable wine-growing practices. This Sauvignon Blanc has delightful lemony aromas on the nose and crisp, zesty fruit on the palate, with gentle richness that makes it a great candidate for the table.

Food pairings: Lobster, baked white fish
Vintage years: 2009, 2008

2 Schramsberg, Blanc de Noirs

Blanc de Noirs wines (cuvées based on Pinot Noir) are a specialty of this producer. Grapes are sourced from a wide range of cool-climate vineyards—mainly from Mendocino, but also Sonoma, Napa, and Marin—to make a structured and toasty sparkling wine that is food-friendly and will age well.

Food pairings: Soft cheeses; simply cooked fish dishes
Vintage years: 2006, 2005, 2002

4 Roederer Estate/ Quartet NV, Anderson Valley, Mendocino

After an extensive search, Champagne house Luis Roederer chose the Anderson Valley to establish the estate that now serves its superb sparkling wines. This cuvée, made from Chardonnay with Pinot Noir playing a strong supporting role, is a great introduction to the range.

Food pairings: Smoked salmon canapés
Vintage years: NV

3 Bonterra Viognier, Mendocino/Lake County

Viognier, along with Marsanne and Roussanne and a touch of Muscat—all organic—make this a particularly imaginative and richly flavored wine. About half the blend has a brief sojourn in oak, giving a hint of vanilla without overpowering the crisp apricot and peach fruit. Delightful.

Food pairings: Salade niçoise, light chicken dishes
Vintage years: 2008, 2007

5 Parducci Zinfandel Rosé

If you think that "pink" Zinfandel is dull, this wine will make you think again. The blend is typically based on Zinfandel, with other grapes such as the floral Moscato Canelli adding interest. The grapes are picked early to ensure freshness and lighter alcohol than many other Zinfandel rosés.

Food pairings: Ideal apéritif—on a sunny patio if possible
Vintage years: 2009, 2008

Sonoma Valley

Sonoma is one of California's best-known wine regions; its association with fine wine dates back to the late nineteenth century. Chardonnay was extensively planted in Sonoma in the wine boom of the 1970s and 1980s, and it remains the most planted grape variety in the area. Increasingly intricate winemaking—and oak usage in particular—has resulted in Chardonnay wines with many nuances and styles and capability of long aging. More recently, other varieties have been introduced that are equally well suited to Sonoma's misty cool climate, such as the perfumed Pinot Gris.

The Frei Ranch Vineyard, Gallo Family Vineyards, Sonoma Valley

1 Flowers Vineyards & Winery, Chardonnay, Sonoma Coast Chardonnay

This Chardonnay comes from vineyards based less than two miles from the Pacific, where conditions favor long, slow ripening. Mostly native yeast is used to make this wine, fermented and aged in French oak. Rich and round with citrus and pear fruit, yet crisp and fresh.

Food pairings: Broiled shrimp, ceviche
Vintage years: 2008, 2007

2 MacMurray Ranch, Pinot Gris, Sonoma Coast

Sonoma Coast is an up-and-coming region for Pinot Gris, which is well suited to the area's soils and long growing season. Around a third of the blend is aged on the lees in French oak for two months to bring out the wine's elegant fruit. Refreshingly different.

Food pairings: Rice dishes, mildly spiced foods
Vintage years: 2008, 2007, 2006

4 Gallo Family Vineyards, Laguna Chardonnay

Gallo's Laguna Ranch vineyard dates back to the late 1800s. Fog lingers here all day, providing ideal cool conditions to grow grapes with crisp acidity and concentrated flavor. A complex Chardonnay with a slightly creamy texture and generous amounts of apple and pear fruit and citrus flavors.

Food pairings: Chicken cooked with lemon and bay leaves
Vintage years: 2008, 2007, 2006

3 Sebastiani, Sonoma County Selection Chardonnay

A blend of grapes from sub-appellations including Carneros, Russian River, and Alexander Valley gives a consistent style. A touch of Roussanne adds interest. Two-thirds of the wine is oaked. A full-bodied Chardonnay with plenty of ripe fruit that always pleases.

Food pairings: Roasted trout with thyme
Vintage years: 2007, 2006

5 Cline Cellars, Viognier

Viognier is well suited to the gentle rolling hills of Carneros, where Cline has established vineyards for the variety. The cooling bay winds moderate the heat during the ripening period, allowing acidity to balance the exuberant tropical flavors and aromas in the grapes. A full-bodied, food-friendly wine.

Food pairings: Baked cod or sea bass, Thai curries
Vintage years: 2008, 2007

6 Cline Cellars, Pinot Gris

The cool Petaluma Gap (Petaluma to San Pablo Bay) has proved to be an ideal location for Pinot Gris to show its true character. Fermented at low temperatures to preserve its delicate aromas and aged for a short period in stainless steel tank. Unoaked and to be enjoyed young.

Food pairings: Smoked fish, cold white meats, salads
Vintage years: 2008, 2007

7 Sonoma-Cutrer, Sonoma Coast Chardonnay

A gently oaked Chardonnay made from grapes from the Cutrer vineyard in the heart of the cool Russian River Valley and select lots from Les Pierres vineyard of Somoma Valley. Delightful fruit in a lean structure—a wine to enjoy now or cellar for a year or two.

Food pairings: Shellfish, fish stew, broiled tuna
Vintage years: 2008, 2007, 2006

9 Littorai, Mays Canyon Chardonnay

Littorai was founded in 1993 by Heidi and Ted Lemon. Ted trained as a winemaker in Burgundy and the classic French approach to the vineyard and winemaking is clearly seen here. Mays Canyon Chardonnay has an elegant underpinning minerality and crisp acidity. Will benefit from cellaring.

Food pairings: Sea bass with whole roast garlic
Vintage years: 2006, 2005

8 Sonoma-Cutrer, Russian River Ranches Chardonnay

A cuvée made from grapes sourced from different lots, vine material, and vine ages, including Owsley Ranch, close to the ocean, and Shiloh in the Mayacamas Range. The oak influence is slightly stronger in this wine, giving a rich and creamy texture and lime and lemon fruit flavors.

Food pairings: Broiled monkfish or salmon
Vintage years: 2008, 2007, 2006

10 Littorai, Charles Heintz Chardonnay

Carefully matching the variety to the most appropriate site—Sonoma's Green Valley in this case—has been rewarded in this wine. A Californian Chardonnay with Burgundian finesse and the sophistication of cool-climate California, and a wine that deserves fine food.

Food pairings: Foie gras and dishes with rich sauces
Vintage years: 2006, 2005

Vineyard in Alexander Valley, Sonoma

Napa Valley

Napa Valley has risen to fame and fortune. The catalyst was the Robert Mondavi winery, which was founded in 1966 with international aspirations when the valley was still a sleepy farming community. Napa's success story is based on high-quality red wine; indeed the range of red grapes in this warmer inland region provides a colorful palette for rosé wines. Southern Napa, including Carneros, can be around 10°F cooler than the north of the region during the summer because of the greater exposure to the Pacific coast. Therefore, most Napa wineries source their white grapes from the south of the valley.

Vineyard at dusk in the Napa Valley

① Duckhorn Vineyards Sauvignon Blanc

This is a take on the classic Bordeaux white style that blends Sauvignon Blanc with a smaller amount of Semillon. Here it works beautifully in a silky textured wine with honeysuckle aromas. Tropical flavors mingle with a touch of spice, thanks to partial barrel-fermentation—very classy indeed.

Food pairings: Pork loin, herb-crusted cod, chicken salad
Vintage years: 2009, 2008, 2007

② Hendry Rosé Ⓡ

A seriously fruity and complex rosé made from a saignée of Cabernet Sauvignon, Cabernet Franc, Petit Verdot, Zinfandel, and Primitivo. It is given a long, cool fermentation and then a five-month rest in stainless steel to allow its delightful summer fruit flavors to evolve. Serve chilled; very food-friendly.

Food pairings: Seafood; alone as apéritif
Vintage years: 2007, 2006, 2005

④ Stags' Leap Wine Cellars, Karia Chardonnay

Karia is derived from a Greek word meaning graceful—a quality that Stags' Leap winemakers seek in this Chadonnay. Various vineyard sources are used, including the Arcadia vineyard, providing the blend with vibrancy and fruit expression gently supported by oak.

Food pairings: Butternut squash ravioli, broiled fish, roast pork
Vintage years: 2009, 2008, 2007

③ Luna Pinot Grigio

Luna now blends a small amount of Chardonnay with Pinot Grigio, giving zest to an already original wine. Some of the Pinot Grigio wine is fermented in "neutral" oak to add texture to the blend. Tangy orange and apricot flavors in a rich style that will last a while.

Food pairings: Oriental and fusion cuisine based on pork or chicken
Vintage years: 2008, 2007

⑤ Hendry Pinot Gris

The grapes for this Pinot Gris wine come from three blocks in Redwood Creek—the coolest areas of Hendry Vineyard. The result is a delicate, aromatic wine that nods to Europe in style. Elegantly made with hints of nectarine and lime flavors on the palate balanced by minerally freshness.

Food pairings: Shellfish, fresh anchovies, fleshy white fish
Vintage years: 2009, 2008, 2007

6 Clos du Val, Chardonnay (Carneros)

As the name suggests, there is French influence here; Bernard Portet established Clos du Val with American partner John Goelet in 1972. The producer's 180-acre vineyard in Carneros, planted to Pinot Noir and Chardonnay, is the source for this very elegant wine. A classic Napa Chardonnay, made for great food.

Food pairings: Baked fish or poultry
Vintage years: 2008, 2007, 2006

7 Cuvaison Chardonnay, Carneros

The grapes for this Chardonnay come from Cuvaison's cooler vineyard in southern Napa. Winemaker Steven Rogstad believes in making a wine that expresses the character of the estate and uses minimal winemaking intervention. Elegant with pure apricot and pear fruit and gently enhanced by around eight months in French oak.

Food pairings: Smoked fish, salads, rice dishes
Vintage years: 2008, 2007, 2006

9 Robert Mondavi Moscato d'Oro 💬

Small pockets of lesser-known grapes reveal California's rich cultural viticultural heritage—the floral Moscato Canelli is a good example. For this wine, the variety is left to ripen well into the fall to make a naturally sweet wine. Jasmine and honeysuckle aromas, honey, and candied-orange fruit with a slight spritz.

Food pairings: Fruitcake or apple pie
Vintage years: 2007, 2006, 2005

8 Ramey Hyde Vineyard Chardonnay

The soils of Hyde Vineyard in Napa's Carneros and careful vine selection account for the superb fruit quality of this sublime Chardonnay. It leans to Burgundy in overall sophistication, but the ripe fruit, gently balanced by oak, places it firmly in California. Carefully cellaring for a few years would be rewarded.

Food pairings: Roast chicken with lemon
Vintage years: 2007, 2006

10 Robert Mondavi Napa Valley Fumé Blanc

This established Mondavi wine is based on Sauvignon Blanc with a small amount of Semillon. The grapes are sourced from the producer's vineyard in various locations of Napa, including Stags' Leap and Oakville. Short barrel aging gives this wine an elegant round structure and dry, savory fruit. Very food-friendly.

Food pairings: Creamy soups, fish pie
Vintage years: 2009, 2008, 2007

Grape picking by hand in Carneros

Santa Cruz, Monterey & Central Coast regions

The regions to the south of San Francisco Bay are not as famous as those to the north, yet some of California's biggest winemaking names are here. They have been attracted to the great variety of climate and terrains found here—particularly those of Santa Cruz Mountains, Arroyo Seco, Paso Robles, and Edna Valley. Once again the proximity to the coast is a major influence. However, temperatures tend to be lower than average for California's vineyards, and the growing season, with little rainfall to concern growers, can be remarkably long.

A vineyard in the Carmel Valley, Monterey

1 Delicato, Loredona Pinot Grigio, Monterey

The grapes for this wine come from the San Bernabe Vineyard in Monterey County, one of the coolest growing regions in California and well suited to aromatic varieties such as Pinot Grigio. Loredona is delicately perfumed with luscious pear and white peach fruit balanced in a clean, fresh style.

Food pairings: Mildly spiced cuisine
Vintage years: 2009, 2008, 2007

2 Hahn SLH Chardonnay, Santa Lucia Highlands

From the same vineyard as its Pinot Grigio sibling, this Chardonnay is an attractive pale gold color with greenish tints. Carefully judged barrel aging has built complexity into the wine, giving it delicate apricot and mango flavors with a hint of spice and toasty notes. A wine that will age gracefully.

Food pairings: Mushroom risotto
Vintage years: 2008, 2007, 2006

4 Hahn SLH Pinot Gris, Santa Lucia Highlands

Hahn's SLH range makes an impressive debut this year. Grapes come from the slopes of its Lone Oak vineyard, where vines benefit from late afternoon breezes. Pure with delicate lychee and peach flavors with elegant freshness balancing the alcohol.

Food pairings: Oysters; spaghetti vongole
Vintage years: 2009, 2008

3 Mer Soleil Chardonnay, Santa Lucia Highlands

Mer Soleil is at the northernmost point of the Sierra Highlands and takes its name from the two most important influences—sun and sea. Chardonnay grapes are vinified and aged in lots according to vine clone and trellis system to produce a wine with sophisticated elegance.

Food pairings: Baked cod or sea bream
Vintage years: 2007

5 Wente Family Vineyards, Hayes Ranch Chardonnay, Monterey

Winemaker Brad Buehler adds a small amount of Gewürztraminer to this Chardonnay, which is made from fruit sourced from the Livermore Valley and Monterey— all sustainably farmed vineyards. Golden yellow, the wine offers plenty of ripe pear and fresh citrus flavors with a hint of vanilla oak.

Food pairings: Broiled poultry
Vintage years: 2009, 2008, 2007

6 Wente Family Vineyards, Riva Ranch Chardonnay, Arroyo Seco

Wente has made Chardonnay wines from its Riva Ranch since the 1960s. The location's cool growing season and deep gravelly soils are particularly favorable for a good sugar and acidity balance. Karl Wente typically adds small amounts of other aromatic varieties to this wine—a particularly rich style.

Food pairings: Chicken with mustard sauce
Vintage years: 2009, 2008, 2007

7 Villa Mount Eden, Bien Nacido Chardonnay, Santa Maria Valley

South of Monterey County, the Santa Maria Valley runs east to west toward the Pacific Ocean. Cool evening temperatures favor crisp acidity and excellent flavor development in Chardonnay grapes. This wine offers delightful lemon flavors and beautifully integrated oak.

Food pairings: Chicken with fennel
Vintage years: 2007, 2006

9 Bonny Doon Vineyard, Vol des Anges Roussanne, Arroyo Seco

In 2006 and 2007 there was a harvest of botrytized Roussanne grapes from the Beeswax vineyard at the mouth of the Arroyo. The 2007 vintage is described as "the greatest dessert wine we have ever produced." Brimming with apricot and honey flavors and remarkable freshness.

Food pairings: Fresh fruit; pastries
Vintage years: 2007, 2006

8 Bonny Doon Vineyard, Le Cigare Blanc, Santa Cruz

Winemaker Randall Grahm can always be relied upon for eclectic wines with generous flavor profiles often inspired by French grapes. Le Cigare Blanc, a blend of Roussanne and Grenache Blanc, evokes the style of the southern Rhône. Dry, invigorating, and very food-friendly.

Food pairings: Charcuterie, ham or asparagus flan
Vintage years: 2009, 2008, 2007

10 Ridge Mountains Estate Chardonnay, Santa Cruz

The grapes for this wine come from vineyards at Monte Bello Ridge, which overlooks San Francisco from the Santa Cruz Mountains south of the city. The most elegant lots were selected after barrel fermentation for the final blend. Deliciously crisp with a hint of lime—very fine.

Food pairings: Turkey; white meats
Vintage years: 2008, 2007, 2006

11 Wente Family Vineyards, Hayes Ranch Pinot Grigio, Monterey

This lively fruity white wine is based on Pinot Grigio grown in the coastal Monterey region. A few other varieties —such as Chardonnay, Riesling, and Gewürz-traminer— make this particularly interesting on the palate. No oak in sight, just a mouth-watering array of zesty fruit in a well-balanced style.

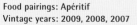

Food pairings: Apéritif
Vintage years: 2009, 2008, 2007

12 Qupé Bien Nacido Cuvée

Chardonnay and Viognier complement each other extremely well in this carefully judged blend. The Viognier grapes are picked at full maturity, giving the wine great aromas, while the crisper Chardonnay adds freshness. Individual lots are fermented and aged for five months in neutral French oak.

Food pairings: Baked trout with herbs
Vintage years: 2009, 2008

14 Alban Viognier, Edna Valley

John Alban, one of California's "Rhône Rangers," has long been a fan of the French white varieties and has realized their potential in California's soils. This wine has great intensity with peach fruit underpinned by savory minerality and balanced acidity. Great aging potential.

Food pairings: Pork chops with apple
Vintage years: 2008, 2007, 2006

13 Qupé Ibarra Marsanne, Santa Ynez Valley

The Marsanne grapes are sourced from various vineyards with careful attention to picking times to ensure good acidity and moderate alcohol levels. Roussanne grapes are also used in the blend. Dry with savory mineral notes, complex, and long. Ages well for up to 20 years.

Food pairings: Roast chicken with ratatouille
Vintage years: 2007, 2006

15 Alban Roussanne, Edna Valley

Another wine with great personality from Alban, this Roussanne wine is given long fermentation in French oak with indigenous yeast. A full-bodied wine with sweet floral aromas, baked apple and dark honey flavors, and a long taste. A very original style that will age well over several years.

Food pairings: Roast turkey or pork
Vintage years: 2008, 2007, 2006

Central Valley

The Central Valley's vast expanse of fertile soils accommodate significant areas of vineyards along with other crops such as citrus fruits, stone fruit, tomatoes, cotton, rice, and cattle raising. Without the coastal influence, temperatures are generally much higher here, making the valley well suited to red grape varieties for reds and rosés; white grapes such as Chardonnay and Viognier can also be found. Lodi, an area to watch for quality wines, is a rich source of old vine Zinfandel grapes due to the higher altitude and resulting cooler temperatures, as well as well-drained soils.

CALIFORNI

Central Valley

●Fresno

Ecological viticulture in Central Valley (mustard flowers between rows of vines)

① Ironstone Vineyards Chardonnay, Lodi

The Kautz Family were the first to plant Chardonnay in the Lodi region, and most of their vineyards can be found in the Cosumnes River subappellation, one of the cooler parts of Lodi. Full-bodied with rich tropical fruit rich tropical fruit and gentle acidity; aged in French oak. A very food-friendly wine.

IRONSTONE

2007 VINTAGE
CALIFORNIA
CHARDONNAY

Food pairings: Broiled scallops
Vintage years: 2008, 2007

② Fetzer Valley Oaks Syrah Rosé ®

Red grape varieties such as Syrah have adapted well to the warm climate of the Central Valley. This is a dry rosé macerated on its skins to achieve a light red color and a structured style. Sealed with a screwcap to preserve its fresh cranberry, orange, and strawberry fruit flavors.

Food pairings: Charcuterie, salads, mild cheeses
Vintage years: 2009, 2008, 2007

④ Clay Station Lodi Viognier

Clay Station is named after a historic stagecoach stop used during the California's Gold Rush. In the mid-1990s, it was established as a vineyard with classic European grape varieties, including Viognier, by the Indelicato family. This unoaked wine offers bright white pear and lychee fruit—enjoy it young.

Food pairings: An apéritif
Vintage years: 2008

③ Ironstone Vineyards, Xpression Rosé ®

This rosé is made from a blend of Zinfandel and white grapes including Chardonnay and Sauvignon Blanc sourced within the Lodi area and from vineyards where sustainable viticulture is practiced. A lively, fruity wine with soft red fruit and crisp citrus flavors best enjoyed chilled and young.

Food pairings: Asian cuisine, barbecues, and picnics
Vintage years: 2009, 2008

⑤ Domaine de la Terre Rouge Muscat à Petits Grains, Shenandoah ⑩

Inspired by the fortified Muscats of France, Muscat brandy from the same vineyard is added to stop fermentation at the desired level of sweetness, followed by maturation in neutral French oak for nine months. The wine's lush honeyed fruit is perfectly balanced by fresh acidity.

Food pairings: Pear tart
Vintage years: 2006, 2005, 2004

Californian appellations

There is a growing trend for California's producers to focus on specific areas and sites—indeed geographical origin is increasingly detailed on wine labels. However, the opposite approach—sourcing (ideally) the best grapes from anywhere within California—can be equally interesting. This greater flexibility allows winemakers to pick and choose according to what each vintage brings and to work with a wide range of grapes or the same variety from various areas. Wine labels carrying the cross-regional "California" description can be some of the most innovative and reliable wines, and they generally come at a good price too.

CALIFORNIA

The Robert Mondavi vineyard—their Woodbridge Rosé is made from a colorful mix of grapes sourced from California's vineyards

1 Delicato, Loredona Syrah Rosé Ⓡ

Loredona Rosé is based on Syrah, with Zinfandel playing a supporting role. The grapes are sourced mostly within Monterey County and take in a diverse range of vineyards. Off-dry in style with enticing flavors of fresh raspberries, cranberries, and a hint of spice with refreshing acidity.

Food pairings: Salads; broiled vegetables
Vintage years: 2009, 2008

2 Beringer Founders' Estate Chardonnay

Winemaker Mary Sullivan selected grapes from two areas for this wine: Chardonnay from the Central Coast for richer fruit flavors and grapes from the North Coast area for crisper apple fruit character. The wine is part fermented to bring out its lively citrus and tropical fruit. A great example of a good California Chardonnay.

Food pairings: Asparagus risotto; smoked salmon ravioli
Vintage years: 2008, 2007

4 Conundrum

This rich tangy wine is made from at least four grapes sourced across California's vineyards (the others remain a secret). They are: Sauvignon Blanc from Napa, Chardonnay and Viognier from Monterey, and Moscato Canelli from Tulare County fermented separately with some oak usage. Lovely intensity of fruit.

Food pairings: Chicken with artichokes and red bell peppers
Vintage years: 2008, 2007

3 Robert Mondavi Woodbridge Rosé Ⓡ

Winemaker Todd Ziemann bases this rosé on Zinfandel. A third of the blend is made up of an eclectic mix of grapes including Tempranillo, Sangiovese, Barbera, and Muscat sourced from Lodi and other regions. A rosé with elegant aromas, ripe summer fruits, and light alcohol. Chill well.

Food pairings: Broiled tuna salad
Vintage years: 2009, 2008

5 Quady Winery, Essencia Orange Muscat Ⓢⱳ

This was the first wine that the Quadys made at their winery at Madera (Central Valley) in 1980; it has since been joined by other increasingly exotic wines, all based on Muscat varieties. Essensia's deliciously fresh orange marmalade and apricot flavors are simply irresistible.

Food pairings: A dessert in itself
Vintage years: 2008

Oregon

Cooler than California, Oregon has emerged rapidly over the last decade as a respected wine region with a very individual character. The wines made here are some of America's most elegant—the styles are often influenced by classic European wine regions, especially those of France and Germany. The state's AVA regions lie principally in valleys between the southern Cascade Mountains and the protective Coastal Range to the west. Most of Oregon's 400 wineries are located in the northern Willamette Valley, where the emphasis is on cool-climate grape varieties: Pinot Noir, Pinot Gris, Riesling, and Pinot Blanc, as well as Chardonnay.

Vineyards in the northern region of Willamette Valley, Oregon

❶ WillaKenzie Pinot Blanc, Willamette Valley

This estate, owned by Frenchman Bernard Lacroute, makes wines exclusively from Pinot grape varieties, including Pinot Blanc. French elegance shines through in a perfectly balanced wine with pure white peach and pear fruit, good acidity, and a long, satisfying taste. A great example of this variety's successful adaptation in Oregon.

Food pairings: Oysters and other shellfish
Vintage years: 2009, 2008, 2007

❷ Willamette Valley Vineyards Pinot Gris

The grapes for this wine come from slopes facing south and southwest in the heart of the valley. Winemaker Forrest Klaffke makes a rich Pinot Gris style by aging the must on the lees and adding a tiny amount of barrel-fermented juice and some Muscat grapes. Good cellaring potential.

Food pairings: Salmon and white fish
Vintage years: 2009, 2008, 2007

❹ Erath Oregon Pinot Gris

Having produced Pinot Gris for over two decades, Erath has a clearly defined Pinot Gris style that reflects the cooler growing conditions of Oregon. Careful picking times and minimal winemaking intervention result in a wine with great depth of flavor. Made for food.

Food pairings: Pork loin with mashed potatoes and glazed carrots
Vintage years: 2009, 2008, 2007

❸ Willamette Valley Vineyards Riesling

This delightful Riesling is made from grapes picked over several weeks and carefully sorted to ensure optimum fruit quality. Both elegant and rich, it nods to Germany in style with its freshness, delicate sweetness, and pure lime and peach flavors. Great choice for those wanting lighter and unoaked wines.

Food pairings: Excellent as aperitif; chicken tagine
Vintage years: 2009, 2008, 2007

❺ Bergström Winery, Dr. Bergström Riesling, Willamette Valley

This wine comes from mature vines in three separate vineyards; each adds a different nuance to the blend. The grapes are picked in mid-October and given a long, slow fermentation. Tangy and fresh with sweet apricot and mango fruit and a hint of lime.

Food pairings: Mildly spiced Asian cuisine
Vintage years: 2008, 2007, 2006

Washington

Washington is the second most important wine grape region in the U.S. after California; its area under vine has grown from 12,800 acres in 1998 to the current 33,000 acres. The state is divided from north to south by the Cascade Mountains. With the exception of Puget Sound, all the state's AVAs—including Columbia Valley, the largest by far—are located on the eastern side of the mountains. Here the climates and terrain of each region can differ dramatically, but an arid climate and long daylight hours during the growing season are common to all of them.

Semillon grapes infected with "noble rot"

① Columbia Crest Two Vines Vineyard 10, Columbia Valley

Vineyard 10, one of the original Columbia Crest Vineyards, is situated along the banks of the Columbia River. Grapes from this vineyard and others throughout the state make up this blend, which includes Chardonnay, Sauvignon Blanc, and Semillon. Vibrant, rich, citrus, melon, and pear fruit in a full-bodied, food-friendly wine.

Food pairings: Pork chops with apple or chicken with lemon
Vintage years: 2009, 2008

② Duck Pond Chardonnay, Columbia Valley

The grapes for this lightly oaked Chardonnay come from the Desert Wind Vineyard. Its location, on the well-drained Wahluke Slope, is one of the hottest areas of the valley, making irrigation essential. Delightful ripe pear and mango fruit with a savory backbone, good acidity, and length.

Food pairings: Chicken with wild mushrooms
Vintage years: 2007, 2006

④ Snoqualmie Winemaker's Select Riesling Columbia Valley

Made from grapes that ripen into the fall, Riesling and small amounts of Muscat and Viognier gives this wine vibrant fruit character with a hint of spice and honeyed sweetness. The alcohol is well balanced and restrained.

Food pairings: Fresh fruit; pastries
Vintage years: 2009, 2008

③ Woodward Canyon Chardonnay, Washington State

A particularly complex wine made from hand-picked grapes from vineyards in two regions: Columbia River Gorge and Walla Walla Valley. The must is fermented in French oak, gently enriching the wine without overpowering its delicious fruit and giving it a smooth texture.

Food pairings: Pork chops with thyme and lemon
Vintage years: 2008, 2007

⑤ Château Ste. Michelle Pinot Gris, Columbia Valley

Specific sites in the Yakima Valley have proved to be an ideal location for Pinot Gris, thanks to sunny days and cool nights that allow the concentration of flavors. The addition of some Viognier grapes and barrel fermentation for around 5 percent of the blend gives this wine an elegant structure.

Food pairings: Chicken; rice dishes
Vintage years: 2009, 2008, 2007

6 Domaine Ste. Michelle Cuvée Brut, Columbia Valley 🆂🅿

This cuvée is a good introduction to the domaine's sparkling wines. It is made from Chardonnay and Pinot Noir according to the traditional Champagne method and spends up to 18 months on the lees. Light, fresh, and crisp with delicate lemon fruit. Good value for money.

Food pairings: Enjoy with sushi or as an apéritif
Vintage years: NV

7 Domaine Ste. Michelle Blanc de Noirs, Columbia Valley 🆂🅿

As the delicate salmon color suggests, this cuvée is made from red Pinot Noir grapes, which give the wine good structure. A lively sparkling wine with light strawberry and red cherry flavors and a slight toasty character. Good candidate for light food and fairly priced.

Food pairings: Smoked salmon or pâté canapés
Vintage years: NV

9 Columbia Crest Grand Estates Chardonnay, Columbia Valley

From vineyards to the east of the Cascades, which block the wet weather coming from the Pacific Ocean. Both French and American oak are used for this buttery, full-bodied wine with rich hints of honey and white fruit balanced by refreshing acidity.

Food pairings: Roast trout
Vintage years: 2008, 2007

8 L'Ecole N°41 Semillon, Columbia Valley

The hallmark of L'Ecole N°41 is pure, expressive wines with character. The Semillon, including some Sauvignon Blanc, is an excellent example. Bright light gold in color, it has a medley of melon, pear, lychee, and lemon flavors enhanced by part barrel aging.

Food pairings: Thanksgiving turkey
Vintage years: 2008, 2007

10 Eroica Riesling, Washington State 🆂🆆

Often cited as America's best example of Riesling, this is a joint venture of Chateau Ste. Michelle and Mosel's Ernst Loosen. Riesling grapes are fermented at low temperatures to extract pure and vibrant fruit character. Sweet with tangy lime flavors and gentle mineral notes.

Food pairings: Thai fish curry with coconut and lemongrass
Vintage years: 2009, 2008, 2007

A giant bottle of Eroica outside Chateau Ste. Michelle

Canada

Much of Canada is too cold for grape growing, but where possible, the country's producers are increasingly successful with varieties such as Chardonnay, Riesling, and Pinot Noir. Wines are made in two areas—southern Ontario, where the Niagara Peninsula is the main wine region, and British Columbia, where the Okanagan Valley is the focal point. Canada is best known for ice wine, an incredibly sweet wine made from frozen grapes with lots of flavor and good acidity. The best wines come from the Niagara region, where the long, warm summers and cold winters create ideal conditions for the style.

A newly planted vineyard in Naramata, Okanagan Valley

1 Inniskillin Riesling Icewine ⓈⓌ

Riesling grapes for this wine are harvested at the end of winter, and a small amount of juice is extracted from each bunch. Mouthwatering, beautifully textured sweet apricot and mango fruit with tangy acidity and light alcohol—an extremely fine wine. Cellar carefully or enjoy well chilled.

Food pairings: Fruit-based desserts, fruit salad, or on its own
Vintage years: 2008, 2007, 2006

2 Inniskillin Sparkling Icewine Vidal Niagara Peninsula ⓈⓅ ⓈⓌ

Made from pressing frozen Vidal grapes at 14°F to extract the juice from the ice crystals before making a sparkling wine. Vibrant gold in color, this exotic wine is extremely rich and honeyed with gentle alcohol. Tip: be sure the wine is sweeter than the dessert, and chill well.

Food pairings: Fruit dipped in chocolate
Vintage years: 2005, 2004

4 Château des Charmes Vidal Icewine, Niagara Peninsula ⓈⓌ

This family-run estate is located south of Lake Ontario and north of Niagara Escarpment, where conditions are ideal for its still, sparkling, and ice wines. The Vidal grapes for this wine are generally picked at the end of January, when the acidity and concentrated sweet fruit has accumulated.

Food pairings: Lemon tart
Vintage years: 2007, 2006, 2004

3 Jackson-Triggs Vintners, Proprietors' Grand Reserve Gewürztraminer Icewine, Niagara Peninsula ⓈⓌ

The grapes for this wine are harvested in late December and during January from specific vineyards and fermented in stainless steel. A fragrant and delicate wine offering delightful tropical fruit and a hint of spice with fresh, balancing acidity.

Food pairings: Pâté; cheesecake
Vintage years: 2007, 2006

5 Mission Hill Family Estate, Five Vineyards Chardonnay, Okanagan Valley

As the name implies, these wines come from five vineyards to achieve consistent quality. Winemaker John Simes aged part of the blend in American oak on its lees, achieving a vibrant Chardonnay with good structure and crisp apple fruit.

Food pairings: Seafood entrées
Vintage years: 2008, 2007

South America

Winemaking has a long and colorful heritage in South America. Vines were first brought to the continent in the sixteenth century by Spanish conquerors and missionaries, and successive waves of immigrants from Spain, Portugal, Italy, Germany, and France have all influenced wine production.

Brazil has a thriving domestic market for sparkling wine, and both white and red wines from the cooler southern regions are on the up—the mountainous Vale do Rio do Peixe region is tipped for great things. However, Brazil's wines have yet to make a significant impact overseas.

Chile and Argentina are the two countries of note for exciting white wines; indeed the diversity and quality of the whites on both sides of the Andes has changed almost beyond recognition in the last decade.

In Argentina, wine producers have taken advantage of altitude, especially in Mendoza, to achieve fresher, brighter wine styles. Modern winemaking and viticultural practices have also contributed to the hike in quality for wines made from the main grapes: Torrontés, Chardonnay, and Sauvignon.

Chile burst onto the international wine scene in the 1990s with very approachable, fruity wines from this viticultural paradise. The country's winemakers are now matching a wider range of grapes to regions never before exploited so seriously. They have moved toward cooler climate areas closer to the Pacific, to the desertlike north—Elqui and Limarí—and south to green Bío Bío. The climate can be more challenging in these regions, but the rewards make it well worthwhile.

Argentina

Argentina is generally associated with very food-friendly red wines; indeed, they tend to eclipse all other styles. Thanks to a wide range of grape varieties—many of them introduced by Italian and Spanish immigrants in the early nineteenth century—you can find some intriguing dry and sweet white wines as well. Argentinians also love sparkling wines, which have been big business for the country for over 50 years.

The country's signature white variety is Torrontés, a highly aromatic grape that bears some similarity to Muscat or Gewürztraminer. Torrontés wines are now far more enjoyable than they once were, thanks to careful vineyard management and changes in winemaking.

It is generally agreed that Chardonnay, especially when grown at high altitude, makes the most impressive whites in Argentina. Barrel-fermentation and a sojourn in oak give Argentinian Chardonnay a touch of class.

N
W **E**
S

 Salta

 Mendoza & Uco Valley

 Patagonia

ARGENTINA

Argentina is subject to
a variety of climates. As
a rule, the climate is
predominantly temperate
with extremes ranging from
subtropical in the north to
subpolar in the far south.
Central Argentina has hot
summers with thunderstorms,
and cold winters.

Salta

Salta, tucked away in the remote northwest of Argentina, is where the Torrontés grape variety excels, providing wines with intense flavor and exotic exuberance. You need a head for heights here, as the vineyards can be located at a breathtaking 3,000 feet, making them among the highest in the world. There are 17 producers in the region, most located around the Cafayate Valley, and many Mendoza wineries make an annual pilgrimage to source Salta Torrontés in the belief that it is the best. Look for young wines and try them with an empanada if you can.

Torrontés grapes do best in the Salta region

❶ Dominio del Plata, Crios Torrontés

An impressive wine made from hand-harvested grapes grown on traditional pergola trellises. To avoid bitterness, care is taken to use clusters that have not received long exposure to the sun. The style is rich and complex with tangy lime flavors and white peach and pear fruit. Deliciously refreshing.

Food matches: Strongly flavored seafood such as crab
Vintage years: 2009, 2008

❷ Trapiche Broquel Torrontés

Winemaker Daniel Pi blends a small amount of Sauvignon Blanc grapes with Torrontés for this wine and it works a treat. This is a very fresh style with delightful citrus and honey flavors, but also rich and round thanks to six months aging on the lees.

Food matches: Seafood, ceviche, sushi, Asian cuisine
Vintage years: 2009, 2008

❹ Terrazas de los Andes Reserva Unoaked Torrontés

After a careful search, the Terrazas winemakers found vineyards for this Torrontés at almost 6,000 feet above sea level. It is white-gold in color with floral aromas and fresh subtle lime and passion fruit flavors. The wine has a screwcap closure to preserve its freshness.

Food matches: Chinese and Thai dishes
Vintage years: 2009, 2008

❸ Catena Zapata, Alamos Torrontés

Catena's chief winemaker Alejando Vigil makes a careful selection of Torrontés grapes during the harvest in the vineyards of Salta in March. This wine captures the full aromatic qualities of the variety; citrus and peach fruit is well balanced with acidity in an unoaked, crisp wine.

Food matches: Chicken tagine, lightly spiced Asian cuisine; good apéritif
Vintage years: 2009, 2008

❺ El Porvenir de Los Andes, Laborum Torrontés

This local winery has rejuvenated 40-year-old vineyards in the heart of the Cafayate Valley and takes a meticulous approach to wine. Its dry Torrontés has impressive intensity on the palate with rich, lemony fruit character and elegant well-balanced freshness. A benchmark style for the region.

Food matches: Asian cuisine
Vintage years: 2008, 2007

❶ ❷ ❸ ❺

Mendoza

Mendoza accounts for the lion's share of Argentina's wine production, with nearly 400 acres under vine. The province takes in many subregions and microclimates as well as around 30 different grapes, a number of which are white varieties or red varieties that are ideal for rosé wines. Despite the aridity of the land, water is plentiful for irrigation, thanks to the melting snow from the nearby Andes. The mountains also make a dramatic and picturesque backdrop to this important agricultural region where immaculately tended vineyards are found alongside olive trees and orchards.

The Mendoza River makes a vital contribution toward the irrigation of the region's vineyards

1 Terrazas de los Andes, Reserva Chardonnay

This producer takes great care to source grapes from the best sites and altitude—Chardonnay grapes come from Tupungato vineyards located at 3,900 feet, giving the wine lovely elegance and freshness. Fermentation and oak maturation takes place at Terrazas' Spanish-style winery at Perdriel.

Food matches: Asparagus risotto; spaghetti carbonara
Vintage years: 2008, 2007

2 Finca Patagonicas, Tapiz Chardonnay

Made from grapes sourced from high-lying vineyards in the Uco Valley, this attractive Chardonnay has a slightly creamy texture on the palate, due to a portion of the wine being fermented in French oak barrels. Delicate apple and pineapple flavors combine with a touch of vanilla in an elegant wine.

Food matches: Fish, poultry, good apéritif wine
Vintage years: 2009, 2008

4 O. Fournier, Urban Uco Sauvignon Blanc

Urban Uco is part of an impressive range from this innovative Spanish-owned producer. The wine is made from a careful selection of grapes grown in vineyards at 3,600 feet in the Vista Flores area of the Uco Valley. It is crisp, lively, and refreshing. Drink young and fresh.

Food matches: Barbecues
Vintage years: 2009, 2008

3 Catena Alta Chardonnay

The sophisticated Catena Alta is made from grapes from its Adriana Vineyard (Gualtallary, Tupungato), one of the region's highest at 4,850 feet. The wine is barrel-fermented and then aged on its lees in oak for 12 months, giving it complex tropical fruit and a touch of spice.

Food matches: Fish stew, roast chicken, light pork dishes
Vintage years: 2007, 2006

5 Doña Paula, Los Cardos Sauvignon Blanc

Doña Paula, a follower of sustainable agricultural practices, chose to plant Sauvignon Blanc vines at its Finca Los Cerezos Estate in 2000 and 2002. Careful vineyard management and winemaking gets the best out of the grapes and the wine style nods to classic French regions—impressive and simply delicious.

Food matches: Seafood salads
Vintage years: 2009, 2008

6 François Lurton, Gran Lurton Corte Friulano Reserva

Friulano grapes from 35-year-old vines are the main ingredient in this eclectic blend, with Pinot Gris, Chardonnay, and Torrontés playing supporting roles. Each variety spends a short period in oak with lees stirring for complexity. A full-bodied wine with rich tropical fruit flavors and a fresh finish.

Food matches: Fish stew, white meat, cheese
Vintage years: 2009, 2008

7 Finca Flichman Rosé ®

Malbec and Shiraz grapes form a great partnership in this deep pink rosé. The style is full-bodied, as you'd expect from Mendoza, with a generous serving of juicy red currant and strawberry fruit. Dry, fresh, and delicious, this is a versatile rosé to be enjoyed with food year-round.

Food matches: Cold meats, salads, lightly spiced foods
Vintage years: 2009, 2008

9 Argento Pinot Grigio Cool Climate

Altitude again plays a major role in a Mendoza white, giving this Pinot Grigio delightful purity and finesse. The grapes, sourced from Rivadavia and the Uco Valley, are fermented in stainless steel, and the wine is bottled young. A dry, refreshing, light wine with crisp citrus flavors.

Food matches: Ideal for light lunches
Vintage years: 2009, 2008

8 François Lurton Pinot Gris

François Lurton's first plantings of Pinot Gris thrived in vineyards at Vista Flores, so he planted more. The grapes are picked during cooler periods at night or early morning and pressed slowly to extract the best juice. An irresistible wine with delightful pure white peach and lychee fruit.

Food matches: Caesar salad, smoked fish, lightly spiced foods
Vintage years: 2009, 2008

10 Marguery Wines, Historias Passito de los Andes Moscato Rosso ⓢ

Moscato Rosso grapes are picked at two stages of ripeness, then sun-dried before fermentation. The wine is pale gold with delicate dried fruit flavors, peach and apricot balanced by gentle acidity and sweetness. This original sweet wine demonstrates the strong Italian heritage in Mendoza.

Food matches: Enjoy on its own
Vintage years: 2008, 2007

Steel tank cellar, Bodega Terrazas de los Andes, Luján de Cuyo, Mendoza

Whites and sparkling wines from Patagonia

ARGENTINA

Patagonia divides into the more established Río Negro at its southern tip and Neuquén to the north, where wines have been produced for less than a decade. These are cooler regions with higher rainfall and strong winds. The soils and climate can be ideal for crisp whites and we're likely to see more exciting wines from these regions in the coming years.

A vineyard in the Tupungato region of Mendoza

① Cavas Rosell Boher, Casa Boher Brut NV, Mendoza

Alejandro Martínez Rosell has set a new standard for sparkling wine. This blend of mostly Pinot Noir and Chardonnay is made by the traditional Champagne method and with 18 months lees aging. It is rich and elegant and a great example of a fine fizz from Argentina.

Food matches: Mild chicken or seafood curries, roast chicken
Vintage years: NV

② Familia Schroeder, Deseado Sweet Sparkling wine, Río Negro

Schroeder's vineyards are located at San Patricio del Chañar in Río Negro. Here the wide diurnal temperature variation favors the flavors and acidity in Torrontés grapes. This youthful, naturally sweet wine is zesty and fresh—a lovely, informal, sparkling wine.

Food matches: Enjoy on its own
Vintage years: 2009, 2008

④ Bodega NQN, Malma Sauvignon Blanc, Neuquén

As a solo act in this unoaked wine, Sauvignon Blanc shows that it is perfectly at home in the south of Argentina. The wine has attractive tropical fruit and grapefruit aromas on the nose, balanced acidity, and a soft texture on the palate.

Food matches: Simple fish dishes and salads
Vintage years: 2009, 2008

③ Bodega del Fin del Mundo, Baqueano Sauvignon Blanc/ Semillon, Neuquén

Winemaker Marcelo Miras believes that Semillon is capable of "extraordinary elegance" in Patagonia. In this unoaked wine it partners with Sauvignon Blanc to make a blend with both fresh citrusy flavors and light honey in a style that will be drinking well for up to two years.

Food matches: Tuna, trout
Vintage years: 2009, 2008

⑤ Bodega NQN, Picada 15 White Blend, Neuquén

An eclectic blend of three grape varieties—Chardonnay, Sauvignon Blanc, and Pinot Noir—from vineyards planted just after the millennium by an innovative producer in the cooler northern Patagonia. A fresh, vibrant wine brimming with citrus and tropical fruit—made to be enjoyed young.

Food matches: Shellfish salads
Vintage years: 2009, 2008

Chile

Chile's extraordinary geography provides its producers with a great choice of climates and soils. They range from the arid north, bordering the Atacama Desert, to the cool Bío Bío Valley, the southern limit for winemaking. Chilled by the Humboldt Current, the cold air from the Pacific is a major influence for white wine areas along the western coast.

The country's winemakers are an experimental lot. They have considerably raised the game for white wines through a combination of improved vine material (including proper Sauvignon Blanc) and by seeking out more favorable locations for varieties such as Chardonnay, Riesling, and Gewürztraminer.

New areas have been explored, not only to the north and south but also west (closer to the Pacific) and east to take advantage of the fresher temperatures of the Andes foothill. Extensive research into soil types and matching grape varieties to them has been carried out along the way.

- ❶ Limarí & Elqui
- ❷ Casablanca Valley
- ❸ Central Valley & South

CHILE

The Chilean climate ranges from arid in the north to glacial in the southeast. The wine producing area benefits from the proximity of the Andes, which create a steep drop in temperatures overnight, maintaining the grapes' acidity levels.

The Central Valley & the South

The Central Valley is the heartland of Chilean wine and home to some of its historic colonial-style wineries. The best sites for white wines take advantage of the cooling influence of the Andes in the east, as in the case of the Cachapoal Valley, or the ocean to the west, as in the coastal area of the Maule Valley. Bío Bío Valley, 300 miles south of Santiago, is an increasingly popular source of Riesling and Gewürztraminer wines. Despite the risk of frost and high rainfall, this area is starting to offer some exciting wines.

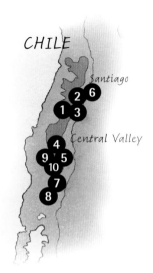

A winemaker picks grapes in Maipo Valley

1 Anakena Ona Viognier/Riesling/Chardonnay, Alto Cachapoal, Rapel Valley

An eclectic blend from a particularly innovative producer, this wine offers generous and rich tropical fruit, apricot, and peach flavors, with a tangy undercurrent and long finish. Around 40 percent of the blend is both fermented and aged in oak, giving the wine good structure for cellaring for a year or so.

Food matches: Fish, white meat, chicken, mildly spiced dishes
Vintage years: 2008, 2007

2 Viña Chocolan Syrah/Petit Verdot Rosé, Maipo Valley Ⓡ

A richly intense rosé in both color and flavor, this wine is made from grapes grown on hillside slopes in the Melipilla region, where nighttime sea breezes favor slow ripening. A fresh, lively wine with juicy red currant and raspberry fruit in a full-bodied style that is very food-friendly.

Food matches: Charcuterie, pizza
Vintage years: 2009, 2008

4 Montes Cherub Rosé of Syrah, Colchagua Valley Ⓡ

Syrah grapes are hand-picked from terraced vineyards in coastal Marchigüe, gently crushed, and given a cold maceration to extract their aromatic qualities and color. The wine has juicy, concentrated red fruit with a touch of spice, an elegant structure, and good length. Decant before serving.

Food matches: Pasta dishes, grills
Vintage years: 2009, 2008

3 Viña Ventisquero, Yali Sauvignon Blanc, Lolol, Rapel Valley

Yali is made from grapes harvested at night from vineyards with a strong maritime influence. The must undergoes long, slow fermentation and is stirred on the lees to release its fresh aromas and delicate lime flavor. A vibrant wine to enjoy young.

Food matches: Light fish dishes, shellfish, Japanese cuisine
Vintage years: 2009, 2008

5 Miguel Torres Santa Digna Reserva Gewürztraminer, Curicó Valley

Torres' Cordillera vineyard, the source for this wine, is located near the Andes—an ideal site for aromatic whites. Riesling is added to the blend to ensure freshness. Intense and perfumed on the nose, the wine is dry and crisp with tangy lychee and white peach fruit.

Food matches: Asian cuisine
Vintage years: 2009, 2008

6 Concha & Toro, Casillero del Diablo Gewürztraminer, Maule Valley

Gewürztraminer is well suited to the alluvial soils of the Maule Valley, as this wine shows. The wine is fermented in stainless steel tanks and aged for five months on the lees, resulting in delightful lychee and melon fruit flavors in a refreshing, uncomplicated, dry style.

Food matches: Fish dishes, Asian cuisine, a good apéritif
Vintage years: 2009, 2008

7 Anakena Single Vineyard Riesling, Maule Valley

The ocean influence and less fertile soils of the Maule allow Riesling to express its personality well in this wine. It has floral aromas on the nose and is vibrant and slightly tangy in an off-dry style, with hints of lemon and marmalade on the palate.

Food matches: Thai cuisine; an original choice for an apéritif
Vintage years: 2009, 2008

9 Torres Vendimia Tardía Riesling, Curicó Valley Sw

The golden color and deliciously rich style of this wine is due to the overripening of the Riesling grapes and botrytis, a feature of the best sweet wines. The wine is aged for about a year in French oak, allowing its exotic apricot and fig flavors to develop.

Food matches: Delightful on its own
Vintage years: 2007, 2006

8 Cono Sur Reserva Riesling, Bío Bío Valley

Talented winemaker Adolfo Hurtado is excited by the potential of Riesling in this cool-climate southern region. This wine shows why. It is youthful and zesty, with ripe apricot and peach fruit flavors, good intensity, and a sweetness perfectly balanced by fresh acidity. Irresistibly refreshing.

Food matches: A delightful apéritif wine
Vintage years: 2009, 2008

10 Aresti Late Harvest Gewürztraminer, Curicó Valley Sw

The grapes were allowed to overripen at the Bellavista Estate to achieve the required sugar level. Each variety was fermented and aged in oak separately before the final blend was made. This intense yellow wine is exquisitely sweet with balanced acidity.

Food matches: Blue cheeses and mature white cheeses
Vintage years: 2007, 2006

Vines growing in Curicó Valley

Casablanca Valley

Vineyards were established in Casablanca in the 1980s, giving Chile her first serious white wines. Chardonnay came first, followed by Sauvignon Blanc in clean, fresh, herbaceous styles to rival the best of the New World. (The region has matched this success with reds, notably Pinot Noir, in warmer sites.) Casablanca's proximity to the sea makes it ideal for cool-climate varieties. A blanket of fog covers the valley each morning, protecting the vines from overexposure to the sun. Midday breezes allow the grapes to ripen without temperatures rising dramatically.

Vineyard of Concha & Toro Wine Estate, Casablanca Valley

1 Cono Sur 20 Barrels Limited Edition Sauvignon Blanc Casablanca Valley

Cono Sur's top Sauvignon Blanc grapes come from the El Centinela Estate in the coolest part of the valley, where the mild temperatures and cool nights enable the fruit to achieve strong expression. The result? Superb mouthwatering grapefruit and lemon flavors with a hint of minerality— very pure, long, and elegant.

Food matches: Simply cooked shellfish, baked fish in mild sauces
Vintage years: 2009, 2008

2 Cono Sur Visión Gewürztraminer, Casablanca Valley

Made from low-yielding vines at the El Marco Estate and aged for five months in stainless steel, Visión Gewürztraminer is bright yellow-green in color. It is dry and slightly tangy with plenty of fruit—apricot and lychee mingle with a soft minerality—and well-balanced alcohol.

Food matches: Best served without food
Vintage years: 2009, 2008

4 Concha & Toro Trio Chardonnay, Casablanca Valley

This is more than a Chardonnay— the inclusion of around 15 percent Pinot Grigio adds citric aromas while the same amount of Riesling adds complexity. Part of the blend is aged in French oak to make a delightfully original wine.

Food matches: Great without food
Vintage years: 2008, 2007

3 De Martino Single Vineyard "Parcela 5" Sauvignon Blanc, Casablanca Valley

"Parcela 5" vineyard is situated on a slope that favors low yields of concentrated fruit with good aromatic qualities. This is a particularly complex Sauvignon Blanc, with delightful citric and lychee flavors, vibrant acidity, and fine persistence on the palate.

Food matches: Asian cuisine; ceviche, sushi
Vintage years: 2009, 2008

5 Viña Errázuriz Chardonnay Wild Ferment, Casablanca Valley

Fermented in stainless steel with native yeast, allowing the wine to develop good complexity and aged on the lees for 10 months in French oak. A medium-bodied wine with a touch of creaminess on the palate, bright tropical fruit, and a slightly toasty character.

Food matches: Baked fish, tagine
Vintage years: 2008, 2007

Elqui & Limarí Valleys

Chile's northernmost wine regions are relatively new to the quality Chilean wine party. The vineyards in the Elqui region have traditionally been used for table grapes and aromatic grapes for Chile's Pisco production. More recent vineyard plantations for winemaking take advantage of the hillsides and reach as high as 6,500 feet; indeed, the scenery of the Elqui Valley is particularly dramatic. Both regions enjoy clear skies, abundant sunshine, cool breezes, and rain-free summers as well as frost-free springs—ideal conditions for crisp, fruity white wines.

Chardonnay grapes in Limarí Valley ripen slowly, due to the cool climate

1 Concha & Toro, Maycas Reserva Chardonnay, Limarí Valley

The fresh breezes, moderate temperatures, and clay soils of the Llanuras de Camarico vineyard provide ideal conditions for this Chardonnay. A full-bodied wine—rich with a hint of fresh fig and a lovely structure, thanks to part barrel aging. Enjoy now or allow to age in the bottle.

Food matches: Fried or baked fish, white meats, salads
Vintage years: 2008, 2007

2 Concha & Toro, Maycas Reserva Sauvignon Blanc, Limarí Valley

Using grapes from the coastal El Tangue vineyard, this wine is both fermented and aged in stainless steel for nine months to allow it to develop its full fruit expression. A refreshing Sauvignon Blanc with good intensity, citrus flavors, an elegant structure, and good length.

Food matches: Ceviche and shellfish
Vintage years: 2008, 2007

4 Viña Tabalí Reserva Viognier, Limarí Valley

A modern boutique winery that has been carefully integrated into the landscape of this arid valley, Tabali's wines express both the grape and the region's character. This unoaked Viognier has delicate white peach flavors and racy acidity with a slight mineral quality. Enjoy fresh and young.

Food matches: Slightly spiced dishes or grilled fish
Vintage years: 2009, 2008

3 De Martino, Legado Chardonnay, Limarí Valley

The grapes for this elegant Chardonnay ripen slowly, due to vineyard location in a relatively cool area of the valley, which gives the wine excellent natural acidity. Ripe apple and citric flavors are perfectly balanced by around 12 months oakaging. A thrilling wine crafted by winemaker Marcelo Retamal.

Food matches: Baked white fish
Vintage years: 2009, 2008

5 Viña Falernia Sauvignon Blanc, Elqui Valley

The grapes for this wine are sourced from the Titon Vineyard, located in a cool area 11 miles inland from the ocean—an ideal site for Sauvignon Blanc. The wine offers tempting tropical fruit on the nose and a fresh herbaceous character on the palate.

Food matches: Salads, roasted vegetables, and light meats
Vintage years: 2009, 2008

Western
Australia

South
Australia

New
South
Wales

Victoria

Tasmania

● Perth

● Adelaide

● Sydney

● Melbourne

● Hobart

Australia

The irrigated vineyards near the Murray and Murrumbidgee Rivers are the source of many of the bottles we see in our shops, but wines labeled as coming from southeast Australia tend to lack varietal character.

In truth, Australia has been so successful at advertising its proficiency in making vast volumes of branded wine that it's easy to forget that some very elegant whites are made in this country.

Explore, instead, the elegant sparkling wines of South Australia's Adelaide Hills, Victoria's Yarra Valley, or the island state of Tasmania. Or compare the elegance of cool-climate Chardonnays from regions as diverse as Margaret River, the Mornington Peninsula, and the Hunter Valley. Semillon can be rich and weighty when it comes from the Eden Valley, while versions from the Hunter Valley are crisp and low in alcohol and those from Margaret River are blended with Sauvignon Blanc to create wines that rival those of Bordeaux with their elegance and complexity.

Aromatic grapes thrive in Australia. Almost every state makes its own version of Riesling, which in all but the most exceptional of circumstances is made in a steely, bone-dry style that works extremely well with the country's Asian-influenced fusion cuisine. Pinot Gris and Gewürztraminer are also being planted with increasing frequency. Other winemakers are exploring the potential of even more exotic varietals, from Rhône grapes like Viognier, Marsanne, and Roussane to Spain's Albariño and Portugal's Verdelho.

While sweet wines are few and far between, Australia's "stickies" (as the natives call dessert wines) are delicious and rich.

South Australia

Many people think of South Australia as being a hot region and therefore unsuitable for the production of top-quality white wines. However, there are a number of cooler zones, often situated on hillsides, where white grapes thrive. Both the Eden and Clare Valleys are noted for their bone-dry Rieslings. Eden is also a great source of rich Semillon and perfumed Viognier, while winemakers in the Clare are beginning to try out other aromatic grapes. McLaren Vale is proving to be a good place to experiment with unusual white grapes. The Adelaide Hills have long been noted for their elegant Chardonnay (some of which is now being turned into sparkling wine) and are now being recognized as a source of crisp, perfumed Sauvignon Blanc. And although it took many of South Australia's winemakers a while to catch on to the popularity of rosés, pink wines are now booming in the state.

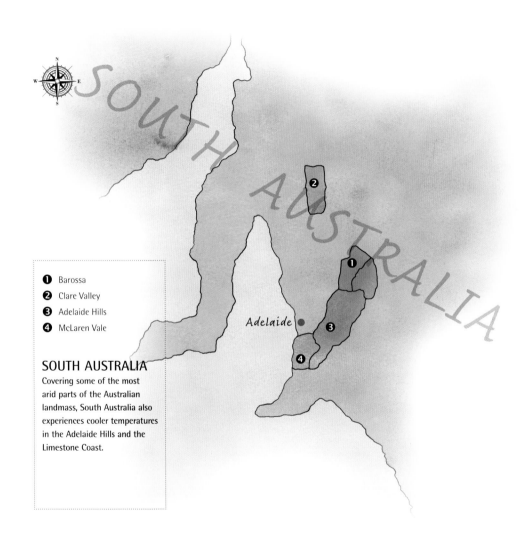

① Barossa

② Clare Valley

③ Adelaide Hills

④ McLaren Vale

SOUTH AUSTRALIA

Covering some of the most
arid parts of the Australian
landmass, South Australia also
experiences cooler temperatures
in the Adelaide Hills and the
Limestone Coast.

Adelaide

Barossa Valley & Eden Valley

The Barossa Valley is Australia's most famous winegrowing region. But although it's best known around the world for its powerful, rich red wines, it's also a wonderful source of aromatic whites and fruity rosés. The rosés tend to be based on Rhône varietals, such as Grenache and Shiraz, of which the region has an abundance. Most whites come from the Eden Valley, a cool-climate ridge that lies to the east of the main part of the Barossa Valley. Riesling is king here, but other white varieties thrive too.

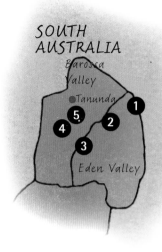

A vineyard in Eden Valley

1 Mesh, Riesling, Eden Valley

Mesh is the result of a joint venture between two of the biggest names in South Australian winemaking, Yalumba's Robert Hill-Smith and Clare winemaker Jeffrey Grosset. This characterful, citrusy Riesling tastes wonderfully vibrant when young, but its fine bones will allow it to age beautifully.

Food matches: Broiled shrimp with chile and lime zest
Vintage years: 2008, 2007, 2006

2 Henschke, Louis Semillon, Eden Valley

Stephen and Prue Henschke make one of Australia's most iconic red wines, a Shiraz called Hill of Grace. They make some pretty good whites, as well, and the Louis Semillon, an intense, concentrated wine that ages well, is a long-time favourite. Great value for money.

Food matches: Roast chicken, rabbit stew, pasta with shellfish
Vintage years: 2007, 2006, 2005

4 St Hallett, Poacher's Blend, Semillon Sauvignon Blanc Riesling, Barossa

In inexperienced hands, this mix of grape varieties might combine to create something strange. Thankfully, judicious blending by these winemakers has resulted in the creation of a wine with attractive tropical fruit flavors and a twist of citrus fruit on the finish.

Food matches: Thai crab salad
Vintage years: 2009, 2008

3 Yalumba, Viognier, Eden Valley

Yalumba's Viogniers set the standard for the rest of Australia. There are three cuvées: the zesty Y series is the entry level and the rich, powerful Virgilius is the top of the range. In between comes the Eden Valley Viognier, with its spiced apricot and pear fruit and well-integrated oak.

Food matches: Asian dishes, such as seafood curries or stir-fries
Vintage years: 2008

5 Turkey Flat, Rosé, Barossa Valley

Peter Schulz is a member of the fourth generation of Schulzes to grow grapes in the Barossa, although he's the first to make his own wines. His rosé is a complex blend of Grenache, Shiraz, Cabernet Sauvignon, and Dolcetto that tastes of cherries and leafy red berries.

Food matches: Fish from the grill
Vintage years: 2009, 2008

Clare Valley

The narrow, twisting hillsides of the Clare Valley are located to the northwest of the Barossa Valley. It is probably altitude, rather than any huge difference in overall climate (which is only moderately cooler than that of the Barossa), that makes the Clare Valley such an iconic area for growing the long-lived, bone-dry Rieslings for which it is famed. The soil in the Clare Valley ranges from iron-rich clay and limestone in the Watervale district to slate in the Polish Hill River district, which has an impact on the style of the wines made in these subzones.

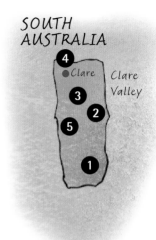

SOUTH AUSTRALIA

Clare

Clare Valley

Pinot Gris grapes on the vine

① Mount Horrocks, Cordon Cut Riesling, Clare Valley (Sw)

Stephanie Toole's Cordon Cut Riesling is one of Australia's classic dessert wines. The term "cordon cut" refers to the practice of cutting through the stalk linking the grapes to the vine, allowing them to raisin in the fall sunshine. The resulting sweet wine is shot through with intense, limey acidity.

Food matches: Lemon or lime desserts
Vintage years: 2008, 2006, 2005

② Jeffrey Grosset, Polish Hill Riesling, Clare Valley 🛢

If the world of Australian Riesling were to have an ambassador, Jeffrey Grosset would be a shoo-in for the job: his Clare Valley Rieslings have both depth and power. The Polish Hill is more restrained and austere than its generous Watervale cousin, but will age incredibly gracefully.

Food matches: Broiled shrimp, ceviche
Vintage years: 2008, 2007, 2005

④ Knappstein, Ackland Vineyard Riesling, Clare Valley 🛢

Knappstein's Julian Langworthy, is an expert at creating intense, elegant wines. This shows only too well in this top-of-the-range, single-vineyard Riesling, which has citrus flavors, underpinned by a steely minerality and softened by delicate floral notes. Lovely in its youth, but should age well.

Food matches: Broiled shrimp; ceviche
Vintage years: 2008, 2007

③ Tim Adams, Pinot Gris, Clare Valley

Since Tim Adams established his Clare Valley winery in 1987, he has acquired a reputation as one of the best producers in the area. Although he makes a classic Clare Riesling, Adams has also been experimenting with other aromatic grapes, and this fleshy, ripe Pinot Gris is a resounding success.

Food matches: Mild curries, Thai seafood salad, smoked fish
Vintage years: 2009, 2008

⑤ Kilikanoon, Mort's Block Watervale Riesling, Clare Valley

Winemaker Kevin Mitchell named this vineyard block after his father, Mort, who planted it in the 1960s. The vines, now averaging over 40 years old, produce a wine of depth and intensity, with the hallmark Clare Valley aromas of lemons and limes.

Food matches: Shrimp with lime, garlic, and chile
Vintage years: 2008

Adelaide Hills

The foothills of the Mount Lofty Ranges are home to the winemaking region of Adelaide Hills. These vineyards, a short distance north of South Australia's state capital, were originally planted in the Victorian era, but their potential had been largely forgotten until they were rediscovered by winemaker Brian Croser in the late 1970s. Since then, the region has proved itself to be a source of elegant white wines, largely due to its relatively high altitude, which helps to create wines of great freshness with good aromatics.

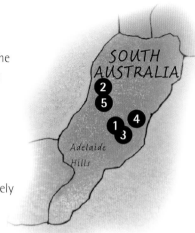

Lenswood Vineyard, Adelaide Hills

1 Shaw & Smith, M3 Vineyard Chardonnay, Adelaide Hills

Cousins Martin Shaw and Michael Hill-Smith (Australia's first Master of Wine) set up business together in 1989. They now make some of the finest wines in the Adelaide Hills, including this concentrated, complex Chardonnay, which is regularly benchmarked against the finest French Burgundies to ensure consistent quality.

Food matches: Roast chicken or pheasant
Vintage years: 2007, 2006, 2005

2 Croser, Sparkling Brut, Adelaide Hills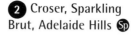

Croser, named after Brian Croser, who first made this cuvée, is based on a blend of Pinot Noir and Chardonnay grown on the slopes of the Adelaide Hills. The wine spends a couple of years aging on its lees to give it complexity and a fine stream of tiny bubbles.

Food matches: Seafood; alone as apéritif
Vintage years: 2006, 2005, 2004

4 The Lane Vineyards, Viognier, Adelaide Hills

Self-confessed bon viveur John Edwards is a larger-than-life character, so it's only fitting that he should make a larger-than-life Viognier. But his wines all have hidden depths, and this one combines ginger-spiced apricot and nectarine fruit with a pleasing minerality and precise balance.

Food matches: Zucchini flowers stuffed with crab, broiled scallops
Vintage years: 2008, 2007

3 Nepenthe, Altitude Sauvignon Blanc, Adelaide Hills

Nepenthe began life in 1994, when the Tweedell family bought 60 acres of vineyards in Lenswood, a subzone of the Adelaide Hills. These days, they make nearly 20 different cuvées, but Sauvignon Blanc remains a specialty. This cuvée balances herbaceous notes with ripe tropical fruit flavors.

Food matches: Goat cheese, Caesar salad
Vintage years: 2009, 2008

5 Tapanappa, Tiers Vineyard Chardonnay, Mount Lofty Ranges, Adelaide Hills

Brian Croser originally planted the Tiers Vineyard back in 1979, the first vineyard planted in the Adelaide Hills since the nineteenth century. This is acknowledged as one of the finest in Australia—a wine of power and sophistication that will develop over time.

Food matches: Roast chicken
Vintage years: 2007, 2006, 2005

McLaren Vale

Nestled between rolling hills and the coast, McLaren Vale is a visitor's delight. Winemakers also find it a pleasant environment in which to work as sea breezes temper the heat. However, it is a region that favors red grapes, so white winemakers need to choose their sites with care to ensure that their grapes don't become overripe and lose acidity and aromatics. Those who get it right are often those who work with grape varieties adapted to a warmer climate—in practice, this means grapes from around the Mediterranean basin rather than those from cooler climates.

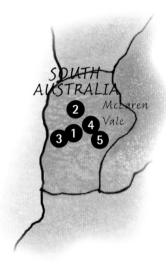

Spring buds on a Chardonnay vine in the McLaren Vale

1 D'Arenberg, Money Spider, Roussanne, McLaren Vale

D'Arenberg makes an extensive range of wines, all as flamboyant as winemaker Chester Osborn's shirts. His Money Spider Roussanne is typically eccentric (it's very unusual to find the grape unblended), yet is still a thoroughly delicious wine, with complex flavors of ripe fruits and spice.

Food matches: Southern Indian-style curry
Vintage years: 2007, 2006

2 Chapel Hill, Verdelho, McLaren Vale

McLaren Vale's Chapel Hill provides gourmet visitors with just about everything they might want: a splendid location, a stunning guesthouse, a cooking school, and a good range of wines. The crisp, clean Verdelho, a grape whose origins lie in Portugal, tastes of gooseberries, lime, and honeysuckle.

Food matches: Crayfish salad with a Thai dressing
Vintage years: 2008, 2007

4 Gemtree Vineyards, Moonstone Albariño, McLaren Vale

Mike Brown has always had a taste for the eclectic, so it's unsurprising to discover that he's an early adopter of Albariño, a newcomer to Australian vineyards whose origins lie in northern Spain. This version is richer than its Spanish cousins, with flavors of pears, dried mangoes, and citrus fruit.

Food matches: Grilled scallops
Vintage years: 2008

3 Linda Domas, Vis a Vis, McLaren Vale

Winemaker Linda Domas and viticulturalist Steve Brunato set up their winery with the aim of making wines inspired as much by French elegance as they are by Australian ripeness. This balance shows in Vis a Vis, a layered blend of Chardonnay and Viognier with opulent aromas but a restrained palate.

Food matches: Asian dishes
Vintage years: 2008, 2007

5 Wirra Wirra, Mrs. Wigley Rosé, McLaren Vale

Wirra Wirra Vineyards were established in 1894 by the cricketer Robert Strangways Wigley. This Grenache-based pink wasn't named after Wigley's wife, but after a stray cat that made a home for herself in the winery. The wine has a creamy texture and lively cherry fruit.

Food matches: Chinese stir-fried duck
Vintage years: 2009, 2008

Victoria & Tasmania

In winemaking terms, Victoria offers some of the greatest diversity in Australia. The cool-climate zones around Melbourne, such as the Geelong and Mornington Peninsulas and the Yarra Valley, offer ideal conditions for growing Chardonnay and Pinot Noir. Rhône grapes thrive in Central Victoria's Goulburn Valley, while the arid heat of Rutherglen enables winemakers to make rich, fortified dessert wines. Meanwhile, the island of Tasmania is proving to be the ideal place in which to make sparkling wine in the southern hemisphere—and it's also a good source of white wines made from aromatic grapes.

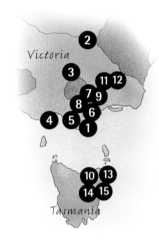

New Chardonnay vineyard in Heathcote, Victoria

1 Stonier, Reserve Chardonnay, Mornington Peninsula

One of the first wineries to make its name on the Mornington Peninsula, Stonier specializes in Pinot Noir and Chardonnay. While the regular Chardonnay cuvée is consistently good, the Reserve bottling is a notch above in terms of depth, complexity, and elegance.

Food matches: Sea bass with herbs
Vintage years: 2007, 2006, 2005

2 Campbells, Classic Rutherglen Muscat, Rutherglen

The warm, dry area of Rutherglen, which lies in the northeast of Victoria, on the shores of the Murray River, is famed for its fortified dessert wines. Campbells Classic is based on very ripe Muscat grapes that, once vinified, are aged in a solera that dates back to the 1950s.

Food matches: Blue cheese, very rich desserts like plum pudding
Vintage years: NV

4 By Farr, Viognier, Geelong

Gary Farr is into making wines that express their origin—in this case the clay and limestone soils of the Geelong Peninsula. In order to do so, he uses traditional techniques in both the vineyard and the winery, and his attention to detail shows in this balanced, elegant Viognier.

Food matches: Lobster, sushi
Vintage years: 2008, 2007

3 Jasper Hill, Georgia's Paddock Riesling, Heathcote

Jasper Hill is one of the stars of Heathcote, and like many of the region's wineries, it specializes in reds, particularly Shiraz. It also makes a tiny amount of Riesling renowned for its concentrated minerality and subtle citrus flavours that develop in intensity and richness over time.

Food matches:Broiled shrimp with lime and chile
Vintage years: 2008, 2007

5 De Bortoli, Yarra Valley Estate Chardonnay, Yarra Valley

This is completely different to the company's high-volume Riverina wines. Presided over by winemaker Steve Webber, the aim is to make "rock star wines" that aspire toward French classics. This comes close to the goal.

Food matches: Salmon with hollandaise sauce, roast monkfish
Vintage years: 2007, 2006, 2005

6 Domaine Chandon, ZD, Yarra Valley Sp

Domaine Chandon/Green Point is owned by Champagne's Moët-Hennessy, but this is no bling brand. The highly respected Tony Jordan is at the helm, and his sparkling wines are among the best in Australia. ZD, which stands for zero dosage, is made from ripe Chardonnay grapes and has a nutty, toasty character.

Food matches: Oysters; shellfish platter
Vintage years: NV

7 Yering Station, Pinot Noir Rosé, Yarra Valley R

Yering Station's slick modern winery, with its breathtaking modern architecture and buzzy restaurant, provides the ideal setting in which to taste its exemplary range of wines. If you can't make it, you could always console yourself with a bottle of this delicious cherry and rose hip–flavored dry rosé.

Food matches: Mildly spiced Asian dishes
Vintage years: 2009, 2008

9 Innocent Bystander, Pink Moscato, Yarra Valley R Sp Sw

This little bottle of sweetish pink fizz provides two thoroughly delightful glassfuls of fun. An unusual blend of Muscat of Alexandria and Black Muscat, it tastes of Turkish delight, strawberry sherbet, and crunchy red apples. A terrific wine for a summer picnic.

Food matches: Ripe strawberries
Vintage years: 2009, 2008

8 Giant Steps, Sexton Vineyard Chardonnay

Giant Steps is named after John Coltrane's first solo album, and it also represents a leap of faith for owner Phil Sexton, who moved to the Yarra in 1997 after selling his winery in Western Australia. This elegant, restrained Chardonnay is among the best in the Yarra.

Food matches: Roast chicken with roast vegetables
Vintage years: 2007, 2006, 2005

10 Pirie Tasmania, Estate Gewürztraminer, Tasmania

Dr. Andrew Pirie is a key figure in the development of Tasmania's wine industry, and this, his new project, is sited in the Tamar Valley in the north of the island. His Estate Gewürztraminer is fresher than many, but still has the grape's hallmark aromas of lychees and rose petals.

Food matches: Mild Indian curries
Vintage years: 2008, 2007

 6 7 8 9 10

11 Mitchelton, Airstrip, Marsanne, Roussanne, Viognier, Goulburn Valley

You'd normally expect a blend of Marsanne, Roussanne, and Viognier to come from somewhere in the Rhône Valley, but Australia's Mitchelton has made this blend its own. It's a richly textured wine, with explosive flavors of melons, peaches, and candied citrus peel, but vibrant acidity holds it all in check.

Food matches: Broiled scallops; Thai seafood salads
Vintage years: 2005, 2004

12 Château Tahbilk, Marsanne, Goulburn Valley

Château Tahbilk, which was established in 1860, is one of Australia's oldest wineries. Marsanne, a white grape whose origins lie in France's Rhône Valley, is one of its specialties—in fact the winery claims to have the largest plantings of the grape in the world.

Food matches: Bouillabaisse; sushi
Vintage years: 2006

14 Jansz, Premium Cuvée, Tasmania 🆂🅿

Tasmania's Tamar Valley has a climate similar to that of Champagne, so no wonder it's becoming such a popular place to make fizz. Jansz is one of the island's foremost producers and oversees five different cuvées, of which this addictive NV blend is the entry-level wine.

Food matches: Apéritif; oysters
Vintage years: NV

13 Taltarni, Clover Hill, Pipers River, Tasmania 🆂🅿

The grapes for this sparkling wine—a blend of 60 percent Chardonnay and 40 percent Pinot Noir—are sourced from some of the top vineyards in Tasmania's Pipers River region. The wine is aged on its lees for a minimum of three years, which gives it extra weight and complexity.

Food matches: Apéritif; oysters
Vintage years: 2004, 2003, 2001

15 Tamar Ridge, Pinot Gris, Tasmania

Tasmania wowed wine drinkers all over the world with its Riesling, and now other aromatic grape varieties are emerging. On the evidence of Tamar Ridge's Pinot Gris, with its refreshing aromas of pears, fresh green herbs, and spice, the island should soon be making waves with this grape too.

Food matches: Smoked fish; roast goose
Vintage years: 2008, 2007

New South Wales

Historically, much of the wine in New South Wales was either made in the Hunter Valley or the Riverina. The latter is a region devoted to bulk production, made possible by irrigation from the local rivers, a fact that is apparent in its alternative name of Murrumbidgee Irrigation Area (MIA for short). The Hunter Valley, on the other hand, is renowned for its Semillon, which has a distinct style that, once tasted, is never forgotten. With a growing interest in cool-climate regions, however, new areas such as Orange and Tumbarumba are beginning to attract attention for all the right reasons.

A small vineyard in New South Wales

1 Tyrrell's, Winemakers Selection Vat 1 Semillon, Hunter Valley

Tyrrell's is a family-owned company that has been based in the Hunter Valley since 1858. Its top cuvées are the Winemakers Selection, of which this is an example. When young, this wine has great fruit purity, but with age it develops Semillon's characteristic toasty notes.

Food matches: Broiled fish when young, roast chicken with age
Vintage years: 2002, 2000, 1999

2 Keith Tulloch, Chardonnay, Hunter Valley

Keith Tulloch has worked as a winemaker at some of the biggest names in the Hunter Valley, so when he set up on his own in the late 1990s, great things were expected of him. So far, he hasn't put a foot wrong, as demonstrated by this powerful, sophisticated Chardonnay.

Food matches: Roast pork with apple sauce, baked cod
Vintage years: 2008, 2007, 2006

4 De Bortoli, Noble One Botrytis Semillon, Riverina

Most of De Bortoli's Riverina operation is geared to producing budget wines in large quantities. The Noble One is the exception that proves the rule, an iconic dessert wine made from grapes infected by botrytis, a fungus that dries out the grape and concentrates all its flavors.

Food matches: Crème brûlée
Vintage years: 2005, 2004

3 Brokenwood, ILR Reserve Semillon, Hunter Valley

One of Brokenwood's founding partners was the wine writer James Halliday, but for the past 27 years, the wines have all been made by Ben Riggs. The ILR Reserve, Brokenwood's top Semillon, is only released after five years in bottle, during the course of which it acquires richness and depth.

Food matches: Broiled fish when young, roast chicken with age
Vintage years: 2003, 2001, 2000

5 Philip Shaw, No. 19 Sauvignon Blanc, Orange

Philip Shaw used to be head winemaker at Rosemount Estate, a big operation based in the Hunter Valley. A few years ago, though, he moved to pioneer the up-and-coming cool-climate region of Orange, where he makes elegant wines such as this intense Sauvignon Blanc.

Food matches: Broiled fish
Vintage years: 2009, 2008

Western Australia

Western Australia is vast, but much of its interior and its north is a virtual desert. As a result, its wineries tend to be clustered in a narrow belt that runs along the south coast (although there are a few in the area around the state capital, Perth). The relatively cool, damp climate has led to a comparison of growing conditions with those of Bordeaux, so it's no surprise to find Bordeaux's white grapes—Sauvignon Blanc and Semillon—thriving here. The temperate conditions also suit Chardonnay and, in the coolest sites of all, Riesling.

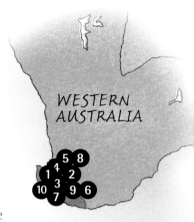

Vineyards with eucalyptus trees, Leeuwin Estate, Margaret River

1 Cullen, Semillon Sauvignon Blanc, Margaret River

In 1966 Diana and Kevin Cullen planted a trial acre of vines. This was the humble origin of what is now recognized as one of the best wine estates in Western Australia. Their youngest daughter, Vanya Cullen, took over winemaking duties in 1989 and now manages the estate's vineyards biodynamically.

Food matches: Shellfish; oysters
Vintage years: 2007, 2006, 2005

2 Suckfizzle, Sauvignon Blanc Semillon, Margaret River

Margaret River is a great source of Sauvignon/Semillon blends. Suckfizzle's version has an intense nose full of grassy, herbaceous notes as well as citrus and gooseberry fruit. The palate reveals a flinty minerality and a rich, creamy texture derived from the time the wine spends in oak.

Food matches: Sea bass; bream with herbs
Vintage years: 2006, 2005, 2004

4 Cape Mentelle, Sauvignon Blanc Semillon, Margaret River

Cape Mentelle is sister winery to New Zealand's famous Cloudy Bay. While it attracts less notice, the wines are just as well made. There's a grassy intensity to the nose of this wine, along with ripe, spicy, tropical fruit flavors.

Food matches: Goat cheese tart; asparagus
Vintage years: 2008, 2007

3 Leeuwin Estate, Art Series Chardonnay, Margaret River

One of Margaret River's top properties, Leeuwin Estate is best known for its Art Series wines, named after the specially commissioned paintings that adorn their labels. The Chardonnay is arguably top of the tree—rich and powerful, yet incredibly elegant and long-lived. This is reflected in its price tag.

Food matches: Roast chicken, turbot, or monkfish
Vintage years: 2006, 2005, 2004

5 Vasse Felix, Heytesbury Chardonnay, Margaret River

The first commercial winery to be established in Margaret River, Vasse Felix now produces around 125,000 cases of wine a year. Luckily, quality hasn't suffered, and its top-of-the-range Chardonnay is potent yet restrained—the wine equivalent of an iron fist in a velvet glove.

Food matches: Roast pork
Vintage years: 2006, 2004, 2002

    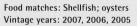

6 Plantagenet, Riesling, Mount Barker, Great Southern

Plantagenet was the first winery to pioneer the Great Southern region. The grapes for this Riesling come from the Wyjup Vineyard, where the vines are nearly 40 years old. The wine itself is bone-dry, with brisk lemon and lime aromas that will take on toasty notes as it ages.

Food matches: Shrimp sautéed with chile, garlic, and lime
Vintage years: 2008, 2007, 2006

7 Ferngrove, Orchid Cossack Riesling, Great Southern

The Great Southern region is one of the coolest in Western Australia. Its warm summer days and cooling night breezes, which roll in off the Southern Ocean, help create wines with great aromatic complexity. This intense Riesling, grown on granite soils, is very pure and long.

Food matches: Thai seafood salads
Vintage years: 2009, 2008

9 Frankland Estate, Isolation Ridge Riesling, Frankland River

This is the most isolated region in Western Australia. This estate was founded in the late 1980s, and the Isolation Ridge Vineyard produces two reds—a Shiraz and a Cabernet Sauvignon—and two whites, a Chardonnay and this elegant, taut Riesling.

Food matches: Scallops with lime, cilantro, and lemongrass
Vintage years: 2008, 2007, 2005

8 Moss Wood, Semillon, Margaret River

Although Moss Wood make a very good Semillon–Sauvignon Blanc blend, its stand-alone Semillon sets a benchmark for the region. The fact that it's not aged in oak allows its youthful aromas of grass clippings and citrus fruit to show through. Age it and toasty aromas will develop.

Food matches: White fish, asparagus
Vintage years: 2007, 2006, 2005

10 Picardy, Chardonnay, Pemberton

Picardy is owned by the Pannell family, who established Margaret River's Moss Wood winery before moving even farther south to Pemberton. Their aim is to bring Burgundian refinement to Western Australia, and given the elegance and balance of their Chardonnay, it may well be that they've achieved their goal.

Food matches: Firm white fish
Vintage years: 2005, 2004

 6 7 8 9 10

Cape Mentelle Vineyard at dusk, Margaret River

NEW ZEALAND

Auckland

Gisborne

Hawkes Bay

Wairarapa

Nelson

Wellington

Marlborough

Waipara

Christchurch

Central Otago

New Zealand

New Zealand has changed the way the world regards Sauvignon Blanc. Although vines have been growing in New Zealand for almost 200 years, it was only in the early 1980s when Sauvignon Blanc was planted in the free-draining, stony soils of the Wairau Valley in Marlborough, South Island, that wine drinkers started to take notice. Here were the sappy, herbaceous, mineral-spiked wines that have become the hallmark of New Zealand and a standard-bearer for this grape variety around the world.

Now Sauvignon represents over half of the wine production of New Zealand, mostly from cool-climate Marlborough, but with other regions such as Nelson, Waipara, and Hawkes Bay also producing good examples. But New Zealand is more than just a one-variety wonder. It has a cool climate, with clear ripening sunshine, providing a long grape-growing season. The regions for growing grapes are mainly on the eastern side of the islands, away from the strong winds and rain that affect the west coast.

The warmer regions of North Island, around Auckland, and Waiheke Island are suitable for Chardonnay, Pinot Gris, Chenin Blanc, and Gewürztraminer. Riesling does well in the protected, east-facing area of Hawkes Bay, while on South Island, from the dry, light soils of Waipara to the rapidly expanding region of Central Otago, grape growers are evaluating and experimenting with varieties to expand their range. Chardonnay, grown specifically for sparkling wines, is important across New Zealand, in particular in Gisborne and Hawkes Bay.

Hawkes Bay & Gisborne

Situated on the easterly tip of North Island, protected from the west by a range of mountains, Gisborne receives a high amount of sunshine but also struggles with rain and humidity. This region is most noted for its production of Chardonnay, particularly for sparkling wine, but other varieties, notably Gewürztraminer and Chenin, are also produced. Farther south, Hawkes Bay frequently records the highest sunshine hours. Its dry climate with free-drained soil provides an ideal location for Chardonnay, Sauvignon Blanc, and an increasing range of other varieties such as Viognier.

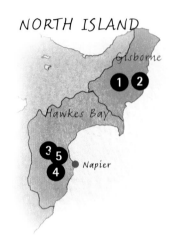

Millton's biodynamic vineyard, Gisborne

1 Kim Crawford Pansy! Rosé, Gisborne

Merlot grapes are sourced in Gisborne for this deep-colored, strawberry- and raspberry-filled fruity rosé with a hint of sweetness on the finish. Kim Crawford is now part of a large multinational company, but quality remains high.

Food pairings: Drink on its own
Vintage years: 2008

2 Millton Chenin Blanc Te Arai Vineyard, Gisborne

The flagship white wine from this biodynamic vineyard on the banks of the Te Arai River near Manutuke. It has crisp acidity to balance the ripe, honeyed pear and quince flavors and just a touch of sweetness on the finish.

Food pairings: Zucchini bake, soft-shell crab
Vintage years: 2008, 2006, 2004

3 Alpha Domus Viognier, Hawkes Bay

Concentrated peachy, honeysuckle flavors in this Viognier from just 87 acres of vineyard on the Heretaunga Plains of Hawkes Bay. Barrel fermentation produces a wine with complex aromas of rose petal and peach with notes of ginger and creamy toasted brioche on the palate.

Food pairings: Baked salmon
Vintage years: 2008, 2007

4 Craggy Range, Les Beaux Cailloux Gimlett Gravels, Hawkes Bay

A dynamic company that carefully matches variety to soil. Barrel-fermented Chardonnay grapes from the deep, stony Gimlett Gravels produce complex wines with lively peachy aromas backed by powerful pear and nutmeg fruit with fine, balanced acidity.

Food pairings: Rich seafood dishes
Vintage years: 2006, 2005, 2002

5 Te Mata Estate "Elston" Chardonnay, Hawkes Bay

Stylish, smooth, polished flavors in this low-cropped, French barrique-fermented Chardonnay from New Zealand's oldest winery. Young wines have tropical aromas of fresh pineapple and peach with oatmeal cookie flavors and good acidity. It ages well for five to seven years.

Food pairings: Creamy pasta
Vintage years: 2008, 2007, 2005

Wairarapa & the rest of North Island

At the southern tip of North Island, protected from prevailing wind and rain by a small range of hills, the region of Wairarapa is most famous for its red wines. However, its proximity to the capital and its dependence on tourism means that grape growers are keen to find white grape varieties that do well in this dry, sunny climate. Riesling, Pinot Gris, and even Sauvignon Blanc are grown successfully here. Across North Island, in particular around Auckland and in the drier climate of Waiheke Island, Chardonnay does very well.

Vines under bird netting, Waiheke Island

1 Cable Bay, Chardonnay, Waiheke Island

Planted in 1998, Cable Bay now has six high-density vineyards on the western side of Waiheke Island. The Chardonnay already shows depth and class with layers of tropical and floral fruit and nutty complexity.

CABLE BAY
Chardonnay
WAIHEKE ISLAND

Food pairings: Cold salmon
Vintage years: 2008, 2007, 2005

2 Kumeu River, Matés Vineyard Chardonnay, Auckland

Burgundy-like complexity and style from this excellent estate west of Auckland, where low yields and meticulous wine-making ensures top-quality flavors. Fresh, citrusy aromas with toasted hazelnuts, minerals, and a rich texture make this one of New Zealand's best Chardonnays.

Food pairings: Roast pork
Vintage years: 2007, 2006, 2005

4 Ata Rangi Lismore Pinot Gris, Martinborough

Late-picked to provide fresh pear and soft floral notes of lemongrass and almond, this is more of an Alsace-style of Pinot Gris with balanced acidity and a touch of sweetness. It ages well for several years, developing smoky complexity.

Food pairings: Lightly spiced Asian foods
Vintage years: 2008, 2007, 2006

3 Dry River Craighall Riesling, Martinborough

One of the first properties to plant vines in the free-draining, gravelly, river terrace soils of Martinborough, this small property has established a reputation for its late-harvest Riesling with orange-blossom aromas and clear lime zest and spice notes on the palate.

Food pairings: Lemongrass-scented Thai foods
Vintage years: 2008, 2007, 2006

5 Palliser Estate Sauvignon Blanc, Martinborough

One of the early leaders in the region and still making quality wines—in particular, this vibrant passion fruit, green herbs, and juicy lime-zest Sauvignon with a weighty, textured mid-palate and harmonious finish.

Food pairings: Tomato-based salads
Vintage years: 2009, 2008

Marlborough

In the early 1970s this stretch of free-draining, gravelly land in the northeast corner of South Island was no more than sheep country. Now it is one of the most famous vineyard regions in the world, renowned for its snappy, vibrant Sauvignon Blancs. Vineyards stretch right across the valley and have expanded into the neighboring, slightly warmer Awatere Valley. Abundant sunshine with cool nights and a long growing season allow long, slow ripening, building the flavors for which this region is now famous. Other varieties, including Chardonnay and Riesling, also do well here.

A vineyard in Blenheim, Marlborough

1 Cloudy Bay Sauvignon Blanc, Marlborough

Iconic and influential, Cloudy Bay Sauvignon Blanc has helped put Marlborough on the wine drinkers' map. Stylishly herbaceous with a good balance of flavors and more balance and weight than many others in the region, Cloudy Bay Sauvignon can even age for a few years.

Food pairings: Scallops in a creamy sauce
Vintage years: 2009, 2008

2 Isabel Estate Chardonnay, Marlborough

Consistent high quality from this large, family-owned property and low yields of elegant, concentrated wines.
The Chardonnay is part oak fermented and undergoes malolactic fermentation to add creamy notes and mouth-feel to the floral fruit and crisp acidity.

Food pairings: Roast chicken
Vintage years: 2007, 2006, 2005

4 Saint Clair Pioneer Block 3, "43 Degrees" Sauvignon Blanc, Marlborough

A dynamic company where specific vineyard parcels are bottled under different labels. This plot is planted at an angle, which gives more shade to the grapes, so the flavors are brighter and more herbaceous than other wines in the range.

Food pairings: Moules marinières
Vintage years: 2009, 2008

3 Dog Point Sauvignon Blanc, Marlborough

Proprietors Ivan Sutherland and James Healy worked at Cloudy Bay for many years and have now escaped corporate life to set up Dog Point. The result is a handmade, small-scale, concentrated, well-flavored wine with zest, balance, and vibrant flavors.

Food pairings: Broiled mackerel
Vintage years: 2009, 2008

5 Seresin Pinot Gris, Marlborough

Organic and biodynamic viticulture at this 11 acre property in the Wairau Valley. Good Sauvignon, Chardonnay, and Pinot Noir, but the Pinot Gris stands out for its generous pear and melon fruit with a smoky, minerally finish.

Food pairings: Cheesy vegetable bake
Vintage years: 2009, 2008, 2007

Sauvignon Blanc grapes—this region is renowned for it's snappy Sauvignon Blancs

6 Huia Sparkling Brut, Marlborough

A traditional bottle-fermented wine, made from Pinot Noir and Chardonnay and aged on its lees for five years, this is one of New Zealand's best sparkling wines, with a fine bead and a soft, yeasty aroma with creamy, lime-edged, rounded fruit and a long toasty finish.

Food pairings: Drink on its own
Vintage years: 2002, 2001, 1998

7 Mahi Sauvignon Blanc, Marlborough

Depth of flavor and rounded complexity in these wines from Brian Bicknall, who for years was the winemaker at Seresin. With a "hands-off" approach to winemaking, the wine has silky soft character, still herbaceous, but subtle, food-friendly, and long.

Food pairings: Creamy fish pie
Vintage years: 2008, 2007

9 Brancott Estate B, Sauvignon Blanc

Brancott is the brand used in the United States for Montana, New Zealand's largest producer and the company which first put its faith in Sauvignon Blanc. Estate B has intense blackcurrant leaf and gooseberry aromas with green capsicum and mineral flavors backed by crisp acidity.

Food pairings: Goat cheese; tomato-based vegetarian dishes
Vintage years: 2009, 2008, 2007

8 Forrest Estate Gewürztraminer, Marlborough

Grown on two sites within the Wairau Valley to give complexity of flavor, this wine is packed with exotic spices, rose petals, and crisp, crunchy, minerally fruit with a rounded sweet finish.

Food pairings: Baked onion tart
Vintage years: 2008, 2007, 2006

10 Villa Maria Reserve Taylor's Pass Sauvignon Blanc, Awatere Valley

A single vineyard wine from one of New Zealand's largest quality producers. This comes from a warm, stony site close to the Awatere River and has ripe passion fruit and gooseberry aromas with a rich palate and crunchy minerality.

Food pairings: Asparagus and salmon
Vintage years: 2009, 2008

Central Otago & the rest of South Island

Outside the Marlborough region, other areas of South Island create their own style of Sauvignon Blanc with rounder, tropical fruit characters. West of Marlborough, slightly warmer and wetter Nelson produces softer styles of Sauvignon, but Riesling is the star here. In the protected area of Waipara, on the eastern coast, Chardonnay is the most widely planted white grape variety as well as Riesling and Sauvignon Blanc. Farther south, in the dramatic landscape of Central Otago, producers are experimenting with many different grape varieties.

SOUTH ISLAND

Nelson ④

⑤ Waipara Valle

② ① ③

Queenstown Central Otago

Riesling is the star of Nelson

① Felton Road Dry Riesling, Central Otago

This biodynamic property in Bannockburn is consistently good across the range, with the Riesling showing particularly well among the whites. Pure, intense honeysuckle aromas with roasted peachy fruit and a clear, dry finish.

Food pairings: Plain broiled white fish
Vintage years: 2008, 2007, 2006

② Mount Difficulty Pinot Gris, Central Otago

A new batch of plantings has taken white grapes over 50 percent at this Bannockburn property. While Pinot Noir is the main attraction, this Pinot Gris has Alsace-like depth of smoky, white peach–flavored wine.

Food pairings: Lightly spiced Asian foods
Vintage years: 2008, 2007, 2006

④ Seifried Riesling, Nelson

Food-friendly wines from this family-owned property in the warm, breezy region of Nelson. Grapes come from two vineyards and are cool-fermented in stainless steel to give bright, tropical fruit with stone fruit and citrus notes backed by crisp minerally acidity.

Food pairings: Seared scallops
Vintage years: 2008, 2007, 2006

③ Quartz Reef Sparkling Brut, Central Otago Sp

A traditional, bottle-fermented sparkling wine made from Pinot Noir and Chardonnay, left on its lees for over three years. The flavors are exceptionally good, with rounded toasty notes and clear, pure fruit.

Food pairings: A perfect apéritif
Vintage years: 2003, 2002

⑤ Pegasus Bay Chardonnay, Waipara Valley

Sheltered from the sea, but close enough to have cool nights, Waipara has a long, cool ripening period, which allows intense flavors to build up in the grapes. This barrel-fermented Chardonnay has lively fruit with spicy, pineapple notes and a long, crisp finish.

Food pairings: Pasta with salmon
Vintage years: 2008, 2007, 2006

South Africa

The old Cape Dutch homesteads—one of many picturesque features of South Africa's winelands—are also a reminder that winemaking here dates back over 300 years to the days of the first European settlers.

There are plenty of reasons why vines have flourished here over the centuries, despite the country's often troubled history. Most significantly the Western Cape has a near-perfect Mediterranean climate with rain generally (and conveniently) occurring during the winter months. Added to this, the three main soil types—granite, Table Mountain sandstone, and shale—moderate vine growth and therefore favor wine quality.

South Africa's early fame and success was based on one wine: Constantia dessert wine. By the late eighteenth century, this naturally sweet wine was recognized as one of the finest of the world. It remains one of the Cape's classic wines today.

The contemporary Cape wine scene has developed rapidly since the door finally closed on the apartheid era and decades of isolation during the twentieth century. Wine producers have taken full advantage of their new freedom, much needed investment has been made, and private enterprise now flourishes in an industry once dominated by cooperatives.

In the mid-2000s the enthusiasm to plant red grapes caused an oversupply of red varietals and blends, but white wine production has now caught up. Pinnacles of excellence are being achieved from old vine Chenin Blanc and Chardonnay, while South Africa has also entered the international league with Sauvignon Blanc.

Stellenbosch, Paarl & Franschhoek

Stellenbosch, the hub of winemaking in the Cape, is home to a high concentration of historic estates and contemporary wineries. The best wines come from vineyards that are cooled by the ocean breezes from False Bay or benefit from cooler temperatures in the hills. Inland, the district of Paarl (named after the "Pearl" mountain) is noted for Chenin Blanc. The Paarl district of Franschhoek Valley has a Huguenot heritage and fine cuisine, set against stunning mountain scenery.

SOUTH AFRICA

The Cape Dutch Homestead of La Motte Old Cellar, proving Franschhoek's history of wine-making

1 Charles Back Fairview Viognier, Paarl

This is a particularly expressive, lively take on the French Rhône grape and a wine that gains character with every vintage. Grapes are sourced from two farms and the wine is part barrel-fermented and oak-aged. Recognizable Viognier perfume with a long, rich palate of apricot and white peach.

Food pairing: Broiled shrimp with chile and lime zest
Vintage years: 2008, 2007, 2006

2 Boekenhoutskloof Semillon, Franschhoek/Paarl

This producer successfully combines original grape varieties and polished winemaking to offer wines such as this Semillon. Lovely intensity on both the nose and the palate, good integration of oak, and slightly waxy, citrusy fruit. A generous food-friendly style that will reward patient cellaring.

Food pairing: Baked cod, fish casseroles, mildly spicy dishes
Vintage years: 2007, 2006

4 Boschendal Classics Rosé, Stellenbosch/ Franschhoek ®

A rosé with an eye-catching cherry color and an equally colorful blend—mostly Merlot with some Ruby Cabernet and Pinot Noir. Only the free-run juice is used for this off-dry, vibrant style, which offers mouthwatering crisp summer fruits. A great rosé all year round.

Food pairing: Charcuterie, duck, salads
Vintage years: 2009, 2008

3 Cape Chamonix Chardonnay Reserve, Franschhoek

The combination of prime hand-picked fruit and Gottfried Mocke's winemaking skill makes this one of the Cape's most impressive whites. The aging in new French oak is carefully judged to bring out the delightful citrusy fruit that gives this wine great finesse.

Food pairing: Roast guinea fowl
Vintage years: 2008, 2007

5 Raats Original Chenin Blanc, Stellenbosch

Talented winemaker Bruwer Raats is synonymous with Chenin Blanc in the Cape. Grapes are picked at different stages of ripeness and vinified according to soil type. This gives a wine with extraordinary purity, overflowing with apple and citrus flavors.

Food pairing: Fish, chicken, Asian food, a delightful apéritif
Vintage years: 2008, 2007

6 The FMC Chenin Blanc, Stellenbosch

Ken Forrester makes this complex wine from low-yielding old bush vines. The grapes are harvested at full maturity and the wine is aged on the lees for around 12 months. It's rich and food-friendly with apricot and vanilla flavors and a great structure. Enjoy now or keep for a while.

Food pairing: Mild curries, poultry, pork
Vintage years: 2008, 2007, 2006

7 Rudera Chenin Blanc, Stellenbosch

Grapes are hand-picked in the early morning from mature vines located on cool slopes in the Koelenhof and Faure areas. The wine is both barrel-fermented and aged on the lees to make an elegant style with soft nutty flavors and tangy grapefruit. Drinks well now but also ages gracefully.

Food pairing: Baked sea bass, Dover sole
Vintage years: 2007

9 Villiera Gewürztraminer, Stellenbosch

Family member Jeff Grier, winemaker, returned to the Cape after gaining international experience. This shows in many of Villiera's wines including the excellent Gewürztraminer. The wine is off-dry and aromatic with fresh lychee fruit, an elegant soft texture, and a clean finish.

Food pairing: A great apéritif
Vintage years: 2008

8 Warwick Estate Chardonnay, Stellenbosch

Warwick Estate is best known for its red wines, but its Chardonnay is consistently impressive and therefore highly recommendable. The wine is aged in oak for just long enough to give it complexity, adding support to its apple and pear fruit.

Food pairing: Baked fish
Vintage years: 2008, 2007

10 Ken Forrester T Noble Late Harvest, Stellenbosch ⓢⓦ

This golden nectar is made from botrytized Chenin Blanc grapes, which are picked over a period of time for a balance between sweetness and acidity. The must is barrel-fermented with natural yeast and aged in large oak barrels. Rich and fresh peach, apricot, and melon flavors.

Food pairing: Berries and ice cream
Vintage years: 2008, 2009

View toward Simonsberg at sunset, Stellenbosch

Western Cape & other regions

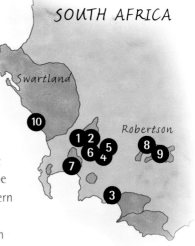

SOUTH AFRICA

Wine with the description "Western Cape" can be made from grapes grown in a range of microclimates, from cooler coastal areas around Cape Town to warmer, higher areas of the Breede River Valley. This enables winemakers to juggle picking times and grape varieties. As a result, some of the most innovative Cape blends carry the classification. Within the wider Western Cape, regions are being rediscovered for quality white wine, including Swartland, an area traditionally known for fortified wines.

Wine-growing near Calitzdorp, Klein Karoo

① Goats do Roam White, Western Cape

Goats really are a charming feature at the Fairview Estate, the parent of this cheekily named range of wines that has been known to ruffle French feathers. This white is a lively blend of varieties including Viognier, Chenin Blanc, and Muscat in a very drinkable refreshing style. Enjoy young.

Food pairing: A wine that gets the evening off to a great start
Vintage years: 2009, 2008

② Goats do Roam Rosé, Western Cape ®

A selection of red grapes such as Pinotage, Shiraz, Grenache, Gamay, and Mourvèdre all bring something to the party, making this a very tempting rosé. The blend is made by the saignée method and aged on the lees, giving plenty of structure. A wine intended for early enjoyment.

Food pairing: Broiled salmon, rice and pasta dishes
Vintage years: 2009, 2008

④ Boekenhoutskloof, The Wolftrap Rosé, Western Cape ®

A thirst-quenching rosé made from a blend of mostly Syrah with some Cinsault and Grenache. Grapes picked earlier provide freshness while those picked later add structure, color, and riper fruit. Strawberry aromas, generous fruit on the palate, and appealingly dry.

Food pairing: Informal drinking
Vintage years: 2009, 2008

③ Newton Johnson Sauvignon Blanc, Western Cape

This impressive wine is based on Sauvignon Blanc from Walker Bay and the cooler, higher Elin region. A touch of barrel-aged Semillon, also from Walker Bay, gives the wine texture, lasting power, and food-friendly appeal. A lively wine with notes of asparagus and green pepper and very well structured.

Food pairing: Smoked salmon, salade niçoise
Vintage years: 2008, 2007

⑤ Boekenhoutskloof, Porcupine Ridge Sauvignon Blanc, Western Cape

This label is inspired by the porcupines that make their home around the Boekenhoutskloof farm. Grapes for the Sauvignon Blanc are sourced from areas such as Malmesbury and Franschhoek, giving this wine plenty of character. Crisp and fresh.

Food pairing: Fried calamari
Vintage years: 2009, 2008

Vineyards in the Tulbagh region

6 Graham Beck Brut, Western Cape Sp

In 1994 Nelson Mandela celebrated his inauguration with this excellent Chardonnay/Pinot Noir cuvée, and now it's even better. One of three traditional-method wines from a producer recognized internationally for Cape sparkling wines. The two grape varieties work in perfect harmony—fresh and elegant with lovely creamy richness.

Food pairing: Duck liver pâté on toast
Vintage years: NV

7 Flagstone Noon Gun, Western Cape

Winemaker Bruce Jack makes a thorough search of the Western Cape for grapes offering plenty of character for this blend, and the components vary according to what he finds. The latest vintage is made from Chenin Blanc, Viognier, and Sauvignon Blanc, served up with no oak, just zesty crisp fruit.

Food pairing: Ideal for light meals and an apéritif
Vintage years: 2008

9 Graham Beck Brut Blanc de Blancs, Robertson Sp

Only the first-press premium juice is used for this Chardonnay sparkling wine. Half of the cuvée is fermented in seasoned oak barrels before reblending with unoaked must and bottling for the second fermentation. Very stylish work from Peter "Bubbles" Ferreira.

Food pairing: Smoked salmon
Vintage years: 2005

8 Springfield Estate, Wild Yeast Chardonnay, Robertson

The winemaking at this estate is as vibrant as the place itself with its delightful mountain scenery, pristine vineyards, and grazing springboks. Winemaker Abrie Bruwer uses natural yeast from the vineyard and no oak, but builds complexity with 13 months aging on the lees.

Food pairing: Cold meats, salads
Vintage years: 2007, 2006

10 The Winery of Good Hope, Black Rock White Blend, Perdeberg-Swartland

A powerful wine made from six coastal vineyards. The grapes come from low-yielding Chenin Blanc vines, with lesser amounts of Chardonnay and Viognier. Well-integrated toasty oak supports this rich yet lively blend.

Food pairing: Roast pork, guinea fowl with fennel, mature cheese
Vintage years: 2008, 2007

Constantia, Elgin, Walker Bay & Elim regions

A handful of regions lining the coast between Cape Point and Cape Agulhas have caused a stir in recent years. Some of the Cape's best Sauvignon Blancs are made here, but other cool climate-loving varieties and both dry and sweet wines can be found. The Walker Bay district has earned a reputation for both Chardonnay and Sauvignon Blanc. Meanwhile, higher altitude benefits later ripening in Elgin, farther inland, and prospects for winemaking around the breezy village of Elim are excellent.

SOUTH AFRICA

Constantia

Elgin

Walker Bay

Elim

Vineyard of Klein Constantia Estate

❶ Iona Wines Sauvignon Blanc, Elgin

The Iona vineyards, situated just east of Cape Town in the heart of this apple-growing region, are heavily influenced by the Atlantic Ocean; there is a favorably long growing period, which is ideal for Sauvignon Blanc. A lively wine with crisp gooseberry and grapefruit flavors; elegant and persistent.

Food pairing: Chill well and enjoy as an apéritif
Vintage years: 2009, 2008

❷ Paul Cluver Weisser Riesling Noble Late Harvest, Elgin

Bunches of grapes with "clean botrytis" are selected to avoid any sour flavors. Half the blend is fermented and aged for eight months in oak, giving the wine remarkable concentration with marmalade and honey flavors in a clean, fresh style. Enjoy now or allow to age gracefully.

Food pairing: Tarte tatin, crème brûlée, cheeses
Vintage years: 2008, 2007

❹ Hamilton Russell Chardonnay, Walker Bay

Hamilton Russell focuses on Chardonnay (and Pinot Noir) at its estate in maritime Walker Bay, with impressive results. The Chardonnay has different nuances in each vintage, but the hallmarks are great fruit intensity, polished use of French oak, and elegance from start to finish.

Food pairing: Loin of pork; chicken with artichokes
Vintage years: 2008, 2007

❸ Paul Cluver Gewürztraminer, Elgin

The grapes for this off-dry aromatic wine are picked early in the morning to ensure fresh grapes and a good flavor profile. Winemaker Andries Burger slowly ferments the must to the desired sugar level and achieves an impressive palate of flavors including lychee and white peach balanced by lively acidity.

Food pairing: Asian cuisine, salads, or enjoy on its own
Vintage years: 2009, 2008

❺ Klein Constantia Vin de Constance

This bright gold classic sweet wine recalls Constantia's glorious past. After a selective harvest of overripe Muscat grapes, the wine is fermented in a combination of stainless steel and large oak barrels. It matures for four years before bottling to produce a rich and complex wine capable of long aging.

Food pairing: No food needed—savor in good company
Vintage years: 2004, 2002, 2001

France

In terms of sheer volume of wine produced, France is the world's second-largest producer. It could be argued, however, that in terms of prestige French wines lead the world. It's certainly true that the sparkling wines produced in Champagne, the Chardonnays of Burgundy, the Sauvignon Blancs of the Loire, and the Viogniers of the Northern Rhône set a benchmark that winemakers around the world long to emulate and wine connoisseurs long to taste. Add to that the country's diversity of white wines and rosés, and it soon becomes apparent that France offers a treasure trove of grape varieties and wine styles.

But the past couple of decades haven't been easy. French wines have been knocked off the top sales spot as people turn to the New World for wines that are easy to drink and easy to buy. One of France's biggest problems is that, although it makes reference-standard wines, its Appellation d'Origine Controlée (AOC) legislation sometimes restricts winemakers in their attempts to make and market their wines. Some have opted to make Vins de Pays, which allows them more freedom, but this is an option only in certain parts of the country.

Even in AOC terms, the fight back has already started, and a new generation of winemakers are turning away from a rigid adherence to tradition in order to make wines that not only reflect their origin, but also give much pleasure to wine drinkers around the world.

Champagne

The most northerly of France's viticultural regions, Champagne produces the world's most famous sparkling wines from grapes grown on the chalky hills and plains that surround the Marne River in the north and the Aube River in the south. The fact that Champagne is made from three grape varieties—Chardonnay, Pinot Noir, and Pinot Meunier—allows for the creation of a vast diversity of styles, from light and ethereal to rich and potent. Most Champagne is NV (non-vintage) and is made using a blend of aged wine and wine from the current vintage. The very best Champagnes, however, tend to be vintage wines made only in the best years.

Wine-growing in vineyards near Cramant, Côte de Blancs, Champagne

1 Philipponnat, Glos des Goisses

The walled vineyard of Clos des Goisses is in the heart of Champagne. The grapes grown here—mainly Pinot Noir, with some Chardonnay—are blended to make this wine in exceptional vintages. This wine is sumptuously potent, and repays further aging in bottle for at least five years after release.

Food pairings: Shellfish; apéritif
Vintage years: 1999, 1998, 1995

2 Taittinger, Comtes de Champagne Blanc de Blancs, Champagne

Taittinger's top cuvée, the Comtes de Champagne, is a thrillingly elegant Blanc de Blancs made from Chardonnay grapes grown in some of the best grand cru vineyards of the Côte de Blancs. The wine is aged for a decade to give it an extra dimension of complexity.

Food pairings: Oysters; apéritif
Vintage years: 1999, 1998, 1996

3 Billecart-Salmon, Rosé, Champagne

This family is famed for the high quality of its rosé Champagne. The top cuvée, the vintage Elisabeth Salmon, is made in such minute quantities that it is near-impossible to find, but the non-vintage has more than enough charm to make it desirable in its own right.

Food pairings: Broiled salmon or tuna; apéritif
Vintage years: NV

4 Bollinger, Special Cuvée, Champagne

Bollinger may well be one of the biggest names in Champagne, but that doesn't mean this family-owned house makes compromises when it comes to quality. The NV blend is always rich and full in style, thanks in large part to the dominance of Pinot Noir in the blend (around 65 percent).

Food pairings: Lobster or scallops; apéritif
Vintage years: NV

5 Krug, Grande Cuvée, Champagne

Krug's "basic" non-vintage cuvée doesn't come cheap, but it's still one of the most sought-after Champagnes in the world. Its desirability stems from its richness and weight, derived from its primary fermentation in oak barrels and six years aging in bottle in the Krug cellars.

Food pairings: Rich shellfish, caviar, apéritif
Vintage years: NV

6 Ruinart, Rosé R Sp

Despite coming from a stable of Champagne houses owned by LVMH, Ruinart has the feel of a small independent producer. Its non-vintage Rosé contains 45 percent Chardon-nay, which gives it a delicate elegance. Balance is made with Pinot Noir from the Montagne de Reims, which adds fruit and complexity.

Food pairings: Salmon or tuna; apéritif
Vintage years: NV

7 Moutard, 6 Cépages Sp

As the name suggests, this cuvée is an unusual blend of six grape varieties. In addition to the usual three grapes used in Champagne (Chardonnay, Pinot Noir, and Pinot Meunier), three more vari-eties (Pinot Blanc, Petit Meslier, and Arbane) have been used to make this complex Champagne.

Food pairings: Shellfish; apéritif
Vintage years: 2003, 2002, 2001

9 Pol Roger, Brut Sp

Pol Roger was Winston Churchill's favorite Champagne house, and it even markets a cuvée named in his honor. The "regular" vintage cuvée shouldn't be underestimated, though. A blend of 60 percent Pinot Noir and 40 percent Chardonnay from some of Champagne's top vineyards, it shows an elegant balance and lightness of touch.

Food pairings: Lobster or scallops; apéritif
Vintage years: NV

8 Moët et Chandon, Brut Imperial Sp

One of the world's best-known Champagne houses, Moët et Chandon makes a range of cuvées, from the Brut Imperial NV to the vintage wines of Dom Perignon. The Brut Imperial, with its lively fruit flavors and creamy mousse, provides a good introduction to the world of Champagne.

Food pairings: Oysters; apéritif
Vintage years: NV

10 Delamotte, Brut Sp

You may have heard of Champagne Salon, one of the most prized and expensive Champagne brands, but Salon's sister house, Delamotte, is a bit of an insider secret. This is strange, considering the high ratings given to the Brut NV by wine critics, but it certainly helps keep the price reasonable.

Food pairings: Sashimi; apéritif
Vintage years: NV

6 ||||| 7 ||||| 8 ||||| 9 ||||| 10 ||||

11 Jacquart, Brut Mosaique

One of the best value NV Champagnes, Jacquart's Brut Mosaique is based on grapes from more than 20 cru vineyards. It gets its elegant floral aromas from the 50 percent Chardonnay included in the blend, and its fruitiness and depth from the 35 percent Pinot Noir and 15 percent Pinot Meunier.

Food pairings: Oysters; apéritif
Vintage years: NV

12 Mumm, Mumm de Cramant Blanc de Blancs, Champagne

Light and elegant, with crisp citrus notes underpinned by a deep, honeyed richness, this is the perfect apéritif wine. Made from Chardonnay grapes grown in the grand cru vineyard of Cramant, this is a really vivid example of top-quality Blanc de Blancs.

Food pairings: Oysters; apéritif
Vintage years: NV

14 Tarlant, Brut Zero

The Tarlant family have been growing grapes in Champagne since 1780. The current generation is firmly focused on creating a range of wines that express their vineyards to the full, including this one, a crisp, zesty wine that has no dosage—hence its name, Brut Zero.

Food pairings: Sashimi, oysters, apéritif
Vintage years: NV

13 Devaux, Cuvée D

While many of the great Champagne houses are based in the heart of the region's grand cru vineyards, Devaux is based in the more humble Aube Valley, where the vineyards are mostly planted with red grape varieties. The Cuvée D is an earthy, satisfying blend of Pinot Noir and Chardonnay.

Food pairings: Rich shellfish; apéritif
Vintage years: NV

15 Charles Heidsieck, Brut Réserve

This is uncommonly generous for a non-vintage cuvée, thanks to the inclusion of a higher-than-average percentage of aged reserve wine in the blend. Another unusual detail is the mention of the date of bottling on the label, giving consumers some idea of the wine's age.

Food pairings: Firm-fleshed white fish; apéritif
Vintage years: NV

Alsace

Situated in the northeastern corner of France, Alsace looks—on paper—as if it might be too cold to ripen grapes fully. While winters are extremely cold, summers are hot and rainfall is low, thanks to the sheltering Vosges mountains. Alsace is best known for its aromatic white grapes, including Riesling, Pinot Gris, Pinot Blanc, Gewürztraminer, Muscat, and Sylvaner. There's a range of styles, including sparkling wines—known as crémants—and sweet Vendange Tardive and Sélection de Grains Nobles style. Beware: Even "dry" wines are not always totally dry—so it pays to know your producers.

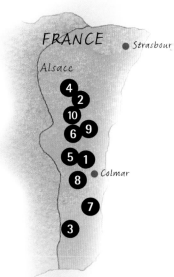

Riesling vines in Alsace

1 Josmeyer, Pinot Auxerrois H Vielles Vignes, Alsace

This wine is made from old-vine grapes grown in the Hengst grand cru vineyard, but cannot be labeled as such because it's not made from a permitted grand cru grape variety. Make no mistake, though, this is a very classy wine, which acquires rich, almost honeyed depths as it ages.

Food pairings: Poultry marinated in North African spices
Vintage years: 2005, 2004, 2002

2 André Ostertag, Sylvaner Vielles Vignes, Alsace

Sylvaner is not, it's fair to say, held in high regard by most Alsatian winemakers, but in the hands of André Ostertag this workhorse grape is transformed into something rather special. Based on 30- to 60-year-old vines, this is a precise and classy white.

Food pairings: A seafood platter
Vintage years: 2008, 2007

4 Marc Kreydenweiss, Riesling Wiebelsberg Grand Cru, Alsace

Marc Kreydenweiss was one of France's earliest adopters of biodynamic viticulture, and his wines show great minerality and a sense of terroir. This particular Riesling comes from a grand cru site and is all flowers and fruit in its youth, becoming richer and spicier as it ages.

Food pairings: Firm white fish
Vintage years: 2006, 2005

3 Domaine Schlumberger, Gewürztraminer Les Princes Abbés, Alsace

This domaine produces fine wines made from the Gewürztraminer grape. This shows all the opulent lychee and rose-petal perfume associated with the grape, but has enough restraint to prevent it from being cloying.

Food pairings: Chinese seafood stir-fries or mild seafood curries
Vintage years: 2006

5 Zind-Humbrecht, Pinot Gris Grand Cru Clos St Urbain, Rangen de Thann, Alsace

Olivier Zind-Humbrecht makes some of Alsace's most stunning, concentrated wines. This Pinot Gris is one of his most sought-after bottlings, a wine that unleashes an avalanche of complex flavors on the palate while retaining a perfect balance of acidity.

Food pairings: Roast chicken
Vintage years: 2006, 2005, 2004

6 Hugel et Fils, Gewürztraminer Jubilee, Alsace

Hugel et Fils is one of the largest négociants in Alsace. Although most of its wines are made from grapes bought in from other growers, the Jubilee range comes from Hugel's own vineyards and is of a very high quality. This is a fine example of Alsatian Gewürztraminer.

Food pairings: Mildly spiced seafood
Vintage years: 2005, 2004

7 René Muré, Crémant d'Alsace 🆂🅿

René Muré is best-known by wine buffs for his Clos St-Landelin Pinot Noir, but he also makes this delicious non-vintage fizz, a blend of Pinots Blanc, Auxerrois, Gris and Noir, with a splash of Riesling. Somewhat richer and creamier in style than many crémants, this wine is the perfect apéritif.

Food pairings: Drink as an apéritif
Vintage years: NV

8 Domaine Albert Mann, Pinot Blanc/ Auxerrois, Alsace

This domaine is run along organic principles and produces a range of dependable wines, of which this blend of Pinot Blanc and Auxerrois, Alsace's workhorse grape, represents the entry level. Nevertheless, it's a fine, fruity wine that is utterly delightful when drunk young.

Food pairings: Fish dishes
Vintage years: 2008, 2007

9 Domaine Bott-Geyl, Pinot Gris, Sonnenglanz Grand Cru, Vendange Tardive, Alsace 🆂🆆

Vendange Tardive ("late harvest") wines are a specialty of the region, only made when the quality is high. The grapes are super-ripe, when all the sugar has been concentrated. The sweet wines are sumptuously rich—a special treat for a special occasion.

Food pairings: Crème caramel
Vintage years: 2005, 2002, 2001

10 Trimbach, Riesling Cuvée Frédéric Emile, Alsace 🛢

Trimbach makes three Rieslings that range from a generic cuvée to the iconic Clos Sainte-Hune. Somewhere in the middle lies Frédéric Emile, widely considered to be a benchmark by which Riesling can be measured. Dry and weighty, with a rich, mineral-laden depth, this is a food wine par excellence.

Food pairings: Spaghetti carbonara
Vintage years: 2005, 2004, 2000

6 7 8 9 10

View of the picturesque town of Andlau by night, Alsace

Jura & Savoie

The high-altitude regions of Jura and Savoie produce some of France's most striking whites wines, yet they are little known outside their birthplace. Both indigenous grape varieties—Savagnin, Gringet, and Roussette in particular—and more widely planted varieties—such as Chardonnay and Roussanne (known as Bergeron in the Savoie)—are cultivated. Local specialties include sparkling Crémant de Jura, *vin jaune*, which is not dissimilar in style to Fino sherry, and the sweet *vin de paille*, named for the straw mats on which the grapes are dried before they are pressed.

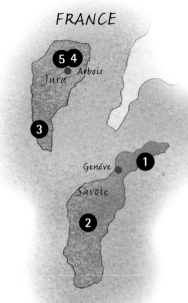

FRANCE

Wine barrels in the beautiful cellars of the Cave de la Reine Jeanne, Arbois

1 Domaine Belluard, Gringet Les Alpes, Vin de Savoie-Ayze

A highly unusual, dry, full-flavored aromatic white made from the Gringet grape variety, grown only in the vineyards of Ayze in Haute Savoie. Dominique Belluard is in the process of converting his vineyards to biodynamic management and ages his wines, in part, in unusual concrete oval tanks.

Food pairings: Freshwater fish
Vintage years: 2007, 2006, 2005

2 Edmond Jacquin et Fils, Marestel, Roussette de Savoie

Patrice and Jean-François (Edmond's sons) make excellent unoaked wines from low-yielding Altesse vines grown on the steep Marestel vineyard. The nose is intense, exotic, and honeyed; the palate is dry and minerally, with rich, spicy apricot flavors underpinned by nervy lemon-tinged acidity. Can age well.

Food pairings: Seafood or chicken stir-fry
Vintage years: 2007, 2006, 2005

4 André et Mireille **Sp** Tissot, Crémant du Jura

This creamy sparkling non-vintage wine, made using the bottle-fermented method, is an excellent blend of Chardonnay and Pinot Noir. It spends over a year on the lees, giving the wine weight and complexity. It is not too tart, with gentle apple flavors and soft bubbles.

Food pairings: An apéritif
Vintage years: NV

3 Domaine Berthet-Bondet, Château-Chalon, Vin Jaune, Jura

Sold in a traditional, short and fat *clavelin* bottle, this legendary *vin jaune*, made from Savagnin grapes grown on steep marly slopes, is allowed to be released only after more than six years aging in old oak casks. Can be difficult to track down, but worth the effort.

Food pairings: Hard cheese, ideally Comté
Vintage years: 2000, 1999, 1998

5 Fréderic Lornet, Arbois Naturé, Jura

Lornet uses the old name for the Savagnin grape, Naturé, to denote his non-oxidative, tank-aged cuvée made from the grape. A fresh, citrus nose with some minerality leads onto a full-bodied palate, with tangy acidity and candied-lemon flavors with a black pepper twist.

Food pairings: Fish, white meats
Vintage years: 2005, 2004, 2002

Burgundy

Chardonnay is a white grape variety that has made itself right at home around the world. It is arguably, however, in Burgundy that it reaches its apogee. Certainly the white wines made in this region of northern France have set a widely recognized benchmark.

The cool climate and fossil-rich soils of Chablis, in northern Burgundy, create the ideal environment for the creation of wines of steely elegance. The Côte d'Or, in the heart of Burgundy, was probably named for its east-facing limestone slopes ("orient" once meant "east"), although many assume "or" means "gold." The Côte Chalonnaise and the Mâconnais lie farther south. While these wines lack the complexity and power of their northern neighbors, they often show more fruit.

Thanks to their worldwide reputation, wines from both Chablis and the Côte d'Or tend to be expensive—particularly if you want to try the top wines. The wines of the Côte Chalonnaise and the Mâconnais often offer better value for money.

BURGUNDY

❶ Chablis

❷ Côte d'Or

❸ Côte Chalonnaise

❹ Mâconnais

BURGUNDY

Burgundy's climate is unpredictable. Winters can be very cold and summers hot, but frosts, hailstorms, and heavy rain can have a huge impact on vintages.

Chablis

Four levels of quality are recognized in the region of Chablis. At the bottom, there's Petit Chablis, then generic Chablis—by far the most common. Further up the scale are premiers crus—about 40 of them, each associated with a vineyard zone—and right at the top come the seven grands crus. The hallmark of good Chablis, whatever the level, is a certain stony minerality, derived from the region's chalky soils and brisk continental climate. Contrary to popular belief, Chablis is not always unoaked —the higher up the quality ladder you go, the more likely a wine is to have been aged in oak—but the oaking should always be done with a light touch.

A pretty vineyard in the Chablis region

1 Domaine William Fèvre, Chablis Grand Cru Bougros

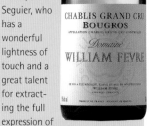

William Fèvre's Grand Cru Bougros always seems to combine restraint with great intensity. This difficult feat is achieved, at least in part, because of the talented young wine-maker, Didier Seguier, who has a wonderful lightness of touch and a great talent for extracting the full expression of a wine's terroir.

Food pairings: Seafood; roast chicken
Vintage years: 2006, 2005, 2002

2 La Chablisienne, Chablis Les Vénerables Vielles Vignes

La Chablisienne is widely considered one of France's best cooperatives. With over 2,700 acres of vineyards, it produces about a quarter of all the Chablis made each year. Its Vielles Vignes (old vines) is a model of concentration and balanced winemaking.

Food pairings: Shellfish, particularly oysters; white fish
Vintage years: 2008, 2007, 2006

4 Domaine Billaud-Simon, Chablis

This family-owned domaine is renowned for producing predominantly unoaked Chablis of great mineral-driven purity. Billaud-Simon owns both premier and grand cru vineyards, but the fruit and zesty acidity of this generic Chablis sets a high standard for others to follow.

Food pairings: Oysters and shellfish
Vintage years: 2008, 2007, 2006

3 Domaine Laroche, Chablis Grand Cru Blanchots

Michel Laroche is one of the region's most influential winemakers, with widespread vineyard holdings. This is a wine whose delicacy and elegance belies its power and longevity. As it ages, those floral aromas develop into something more earthy and truffled.

Food pairings: Shellfish and white fish (younger vintages); wild mushroom risotto (older vintages)
Vintage years: 2006, 2002, 2001

5 Domaine Seguinot-Bordet, Petit Chablis

There's a lot of dilute, bland Petit Chablis on the market, but not here. In terms of entry-level Chablis, this wine regularly over-performs. With its delicate floral and citrus aromas, this is not a wine that ages well, but it does give considerable pleasure in its fresh, lively youth.

Food pairings: Oysters and shellfish
Vintage years: 2008, 2007

6 Gérard Tremblay, Chablis

Gérard Tremblay is another of Chablis' superstars, with a roster of wines from starry premier and grand cru vineyards. The domaine's basic Chablis, however, shouldn't be overlooked —especially when you're looking for a classic, refreshing, citrus-scented Chablis to wash down a platter of oysters.

Food pairings: Shellfish, particularly oysters
Vintage years: 2008, 2007, 2006

7 Jean-Claude Bessin, Chablis 1er Cru Montmains

This former architect and his wife inherited a few acres of Chablis vineyards a couple of decades ago. Their empire now includes acreage in premier and grand cru zones. This has great purity, with expressive minerality and a honeyed note that becomes richer and more pronounced with age.

Food pairings: Seafood
Vintage years: 2006, 2005, 2002

9 Jean-Marc Brocard, Chablis Vielles Vignes Domaine Sainte Claire

Since the early 1970s, Brocard has expanded his winemaking enterprise to some 1,450 acres around Burgundy. Chablis, however, is at its heart, and the old vines referred to in the name of this wine are around 60 years old, giving this cuvée more depth and concentration than most.

Food pairings: Delicate white fish
Vintage years: 2007, 2006, 2004

8 Château Long-Depaquit, Grand Cru La Moutonne

This château's history dates back to the French Revolution, although its vineyards were cultivated in the medieval era by the monks of Abbey of Pontigny. Its top cuvée is La Moutonne, whose vines straddle the grand cru vineyards of Les Preuses and Les Vaudésirs.

Food pairings: Turbot
Vintage years: 2006, 2005, 2002

10 Domaine Raveneau, Chablis 1er Cru, Montée de Tonnerre

Jean-Marie and Bernard Raveneau make what can only be described as cult wines from 185 acres of premier and grand cru sites. There's a tension to all of their wines that, after aging at least five years, enables them to reveal their full, layered complexity.

Food pairings: Firm white fish
Vintage years: 2006, 2005, 2002

A vineyard on a golden fall day in Chablis

Côte d'Or

The Côte d'Or is one of the most complex wine-growing regions in the world as well as one of the most hallowed. Its vineyards are divided into a patchwork of generic, Village, Premier, and Grand Cru zones, then further fragmented because individual holdings are small. To complicate matters further, the climate in the Côte d'Or is highly variable, making vintage an important factor in any wine-buying decision. The Côte d'Or can be split into the Côte de Nuits in the north (mainly planted with Pinot Noir) and the Côte de Beaune to the south (planted with both Pinot Noir and Chardonnay).

A view over the vineyards from the wine village of Meursault

1 Maison Deux Montille, 1er Cru Poruzots, Meursault

Good Burgundy, sadly, doesn't come cheap, but while Maison Deux Montille's Poruzots is expensive, other producers' wines from this vineyard tend to be even more so. So, in a way, this wine is a bargain. Savor its concentrated richness and chiseled profile when you want to celebrate.

Food pairings: Firm fleshed white fish; lobster
Vintage years: 2006, 2005, 2002

2 Château de Puligny–Montrachet, Puligny–Montrachet

This domaine is run along organic and biodynamic principles, with the aim of creating wines with a sense of origin. Its Puligny-Montrachet is rich and opulent, while still maintaining a streak of vivid acidity that prevents it from ever becoming cloying.

Food pairings: Crayfish or lobster
Vintage years: 2006, 2005, 2002

4 Maison Louis Jadot, Saint-Aubin

Saint-Aubin wines are often referred to as being "mini Puligny-Montrachets," thanks to their full-bodied roundness and ripe aromas of peach and hazelnuts. This particular version, a classic reflection of the wines from this appellation, is made by Maison Louis Jadot, one of Burgundy's biggest négociant houses.

Food pairings: Roast pork
Vintage years: 2008, 2007, 2006

3 Etienne Sauzet, Bourgogne Blanc

Etienne Sauzet specializes in wines from premier and grand cru vineyards, but also makes an entry-level cuvée, which sometimes goes by the name "La Tufera." It is a very complete and pleasing regional Burgundy, with just a little oak to round out any lean edges. Great value for money.

Food pairings: Roast chicken
Vintage years: 2007, 2006, 2005

5 Anne Gros, Cuvée Marine, Haute Côtes de Nuits Blanc

A rare exception to the rule that the Côte de Nuits is chiefly a source of red wines, this wine is made from Chardonnay grown just above the village of Vosne-Romanée. It isn't intended to be a long-lived cuvée; drink it young to enjoy citrus flavors.

Food pairings: Broiled vegetables; delicate white fish
Vintage years: 2007, 2006

6 Domaine Gerard Chavy, 1er Cru Les Folatières, Puligny-Montrachet

This family-owned winery is focused on the production of 1er Cru Puligny-Montrachets. The Chavy brothers are rising stars of the region, but prices are reasonable for wines of this quality. The Folatières is restrained and concentrated and should age well. (Sold as Domaine Alain Chavy from 2006.)

Food pairings: Poached salmon, preferably wild
Vintage years: 2006, 2005, 2002

7 Jean-Philippe Fichet, Les Tessons, Meursault

One of Burgundy's rising stars, most of Fichet's wines come from Meursault. Although they are only of Village level, he vinifies his vineyard parcels separately to highlight their differences. All his wines are far less rich and oaky than traditional Meursaults, as shown by the seamless pure fruit of his Tessons.

Food pairings: Roast pork
Vintage years: 2006, 2005, 2002

9 Bouchard Père et Fils, 1er Cru Les Genevrières, Meursault 🛢

The quality here has improved dramatically since it was taken over in the mid-1990s by Champagne house Henriot. Meursault is a particular strength—Bouchard owns a number of 1er cru vineyards—and Les Genevrières is a favorite, thanks to its depth and richness.

Food pairings: Broiled lobster
Vintage years: 2006, 2005, 2002

8 Bernard Morey, Vielles Vignes, Chassagne-Montrachet

Morey is regarded as one of the appellation's key producers. His wines have lots of ripe up-front fruit, but there's plenty of acidity and minerality to keep everything in check. This wine is a Village-level bottling, but gives an idea of the power and concentration of Morey's premier crus.

Food pairings: Broiled lobster
Vintage years: 2006, 2005, 2002

10 Vincent Dancer, 1er Cru Tête du Clos, Chassagne-Montrachet 🛢

Vincent Dancer, one of Burgundy's young guns, has a reputation for being a bit of a perfectionist. This certainly shows in the powerful steeliness of this premier cru from Chassagne-Montrachet. This is a wine that reveals itself at its best only after several years in bottle.

Food pairings: Roast chicken
Vintage years: 2007, 2006, 2002

Crates of freshly picked Chardonnay grapes, Burgundy

Côte Chalonnaise

With its northern tip just across the N74 from the prestigious vineyards of Chassagne-Montrachet, it seems incredible that the wines of the Côte Chalonnaise should taste so different. The difference lies in its climate, rather than its soil, which is still based on limestone. The higher altitude, however, of the Chalonnaise vineyards means that the grapes take longer to ripen than those of the Côte d'Or, resulting in leaner wines with less rich fruit and higher levels of acidity. Both reds and whites are made here; most are based on Pinot Noir and Chardonnay. The exception is the appellation of Bouzeron, whose white wines are made from the Aligoté grape.

Rows of vines, Côte Chalonnaise

① Joseph Drouhin, Blanc, Rully

One of the best-known négociants in Burgundy, with a portfolio of wines covering most of the region's big-ticket appellations. If you can't buy into Montrachet, however, take a look at this Village-level Rully, which offers great value for money, along with a zingy palate perfumed with crisp green apples.

Food pairings: Seafood
Vintage years: 2007, 2006, 2005

② Domaine Ninot, 1er Cru Grésigny, Rully

The youthful Erell Ninot is in control of her family's centuries-old grape-growing operation. She's clearly a steady hand on the tiller, as evidenced by the quality and purity of this Rully Premier Cru. Age the wine for a couple of years to allow it to lose its adolescent angularity.

Food pairings: Vegetarian dishes
Vintage years: 2007, 2006, 2005

④ Domaine de Villaine, Aligoté, Bouzeron

Aubert de Villaine is co-owner of the famous Domaine du Romanée-Conti, whose red wines sell for a king's ransom. Here, in the humble village of Bouzeron, he makes a crisp citrus-scented wine from the local Aligoté. This unpretentious wine shows why he is so highly regarded.

Food pairings: Seafood
Vintage years: 2007, 2006, 2005

③ Olivier Leflaive, 1er Cru Rabourcé, Rully

Olivier Leflaive makes note-worthy wines from a huge number of different appellations across Burgundy. This cuvée is something of a flagship for the appellation. Its south-facing vines ensure consistent ripening from one vintage to the next, guaranteeing the wines a rich texture and weight.

Food pairings: Roast chicken
Vintage years: 2007, 2006, 2005

⑤ Louis Latour, 1er Cru La Grande Roche, Montagny

In the far south of the region, the appellation of Montagny makes wines with slightly more body and depth than the average for this appellation. This wine comes from a vineyard high up on the slopes of Montagny, so it's full of ripe, buttery fruit.

Food pairings: Fish in cream sauce
Vintage years: 2007, 2006, 2005

Mâconnais

The Mâconnais region lies in the far south of the Burgundy region (its southern tip abuts the vineyards of Beaujolais). Its rolling limestone hills make it ideal for growing Chardonnay, and white wines account for two-thirds of the local production. Most Mâcon is labeled as either generic Mâcon or Mâcon Villages. In some instances, the village in question is named—for instance, Mâcon-Lugny. Appellations such as Pouilly-Fuissé, St-Véran, and Viré-Clessé also belong to the Mâconnais family. As always in France, the name of a village is supposed to confer a guarantee of higher quality than wines of the generic appellation, although it still pays to find a good producer.

The Rock of Solutré in the heart of the Pouilly-Fuissé appellation

1 Jean Thévenet, Domaine de la Bongran, Mâcon-Villages

Jean Thévenet believes in doing things his own way. A refusal to stick to the appellation rules has meant that this, his top cuvée, has been denied AOC Viré-Clessé status. No matter, his wines have their fans— and a sip of this striking, honeyed white reveals just why that is.

Food pairings: Roast pork with a fruity sauce
Vintage years: 2002, 2001

2 Domaine Cordier, Vers Cras, Pouilly-Fuissé

The whites of Pouilly-Fuissé come at a premium in terms of price, thanks in part to their high quality and in part to their critical acclaim. Cordier's wines tend to be super-ripe, but the Vers Cras gives an overall impression of profound balance. Even better after a few years in bottle.

Food pairings: White fish
Vintage years: 2006, 2005, 2002

4 Domaine Eric Forest, La Côte, Pouilly-Fuissé

La Côte is one of the highest vineyards of this appellation. Its limestone soil contains a seam of clay that lends concentration and power to this precise, vibrant wine. Although it is a lovely, refreshing drink when young, a couple of years in bottle will help it reveal itself to the fullest.

Food pairings: Roast chicken in a creamy sauce
Vintage years: 2007, 2006, 2005

3 Les Héritiers du Comte Lafon, Clos du Four, Mâcon-Milly Lamartine

Dominique Lafon's Meursaults attract a good deal of critical attention, but his wines from the Mâconnais are almost as highly rated. This is the pick of the crop; a rich wine with a distinct streak of minerality along with a ripe, honeyed note.

Food pairings: Chicken dishes
Vintage years: 2007, 2006, 2005

5 Jacques et Nathalie Saumaize, En Crèches, St-Véran

The wines of St-Véran tend to have more staying power than most Mâconnais wines, but perhaps without the depth and longevity of those of Pouilly-Fuissé. This particular cuvée is vinified in stainless steel, ensuring lively fruit with a streak of limpid acidity. Best drunk young.

Food pairings: White fish
Vintage years: 2007, 2006, 2005

Loire

The Loire is France's largest producer of white wines as well as its second-largest producer of sparkling wines and the origin of a range of rosés. The region's whites are wonderfully diverse, ranging from bone-dry through to lusciously sweet. What they have in common is a marvelously refreshing thread of acidity that gives even the sweetest wines drinkability. Loire wines usually offer great value, too.

The three main grape varieties are Melon de Bourgogne, which is grown close to the Atlantic; Chenin Blanc in Anjou-Saumur and Touraine; and Sauvignon Blanc from eastern Touraine to Sancerre and Pouilly. Chardonnay is a minor variety, chiefly used in sparkling wines.

Soils in the Loire range from sand and clay to chalky *tuffeau*, gravel, and flint-rich silex. The climate is similarly diverse, with the coastal areas being warmed by the Gulf Stream, while more extreme continental conditions prevail inland.

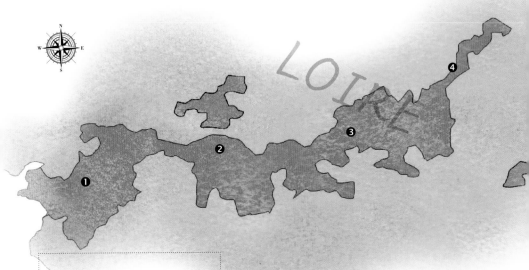

❶ Pays Nantais

❷ Anjou-Saumur
❸ Touraine
❹ Upper Loire

LOIRE

The Loire river has profound impact on
the region's climate, tempering the inland
continental climate by a few degrees. It also
provides the perfect conditions for producing
the region's dessert wines.

Pays Nantais

This is the land of fish-loving Muscadet, easily the Loire's largest appellation, with 31,863 vineyard acres of early-ripening Melon de Bourgogne—the sole grape used for making Muscadet. There are three subzones, and of these Muscadet de Sèvre-et-Maine is easily the most important. Look for sur lie wines; these are bottled straight off the lees, which give the wines more weight and freshness. The quality of Muscadet has improved enormously over the past ten years and is now often a real bargain. Muscadets from top-quality producers age well and develop further complexity.

Muscadet vineyard, Pays Nantais

1 Château du Cléray, Muscadet de Sèvre-et-Maine sur lie

Although the property was recently bought by Grands Chais de France, the wine is still made by Pierre Sauvion, the son of one of the previous owners. Classic Muscadet with lightly floral aromas, lemony weight, and mineral finish, with just a slight prickle on the tongue from the lees aging.

Food pairings: Seafood platter
Vintage years: 2007, 2006, 2005

2 Domaine Luneau-Papin, Clos des Allées, Muscadet de Sèvre-et-Maine sur lie

A meticulous producer who vinifies his Muscadets according to their different soils. This vineyard is planted on mica-schist and produces particularly pure, mineral wines. These wines have the capacity to age at least a decade.

Food pairings: Broiled shrimp (younger vintages), fish with beurre blanc (older vintages)
Vintage years: 2007, 2006, 2005

4 Domaine des Herbauges, Clos de la Fine, Muscadet Coteaux du Grand-Lieu

This deliciously creamy wine with a lemon and mineral aftertaste comes from the largest estate in the small Muscadet zone around the Lac de Grandlieu. Jérome Choblet now puts all of his Muscadet into screwcap, one of the few Loire producers who do so.

Food pairings: Broiled sea bass
Vintage years: 2007, 2006

3 Chéreau-Carré, Château de Chasseloir, Cuvée de Ceps Centenaire, Muscadet de Sèvre-et-Maine

Made exclusively from a parcel of vines whose average age is more than 100 years old, this has long been one of the region's most admired wines. The old vines give the wine both lemony concentration and a long mineral finish.

Food pairings: Broiled sole; crayfish
Vintage years: 2003

5 Domaine Saint-Nicolas, Les Clous, Fiefs Vendéens

Saint-Nicolas is a biodynamic estate in Brem, close to the tourist beaches of the Vendée. Les Clous is a blend of 50 percent Chenin Blanc and 50 percent Chardonnay. This has melony and peachy fruit, with honeyed tones developing as the wine ages.

Food pairings: Poultry in white sauce
Vintage years: 2007, 2006, 2005

Anjou-Saumur

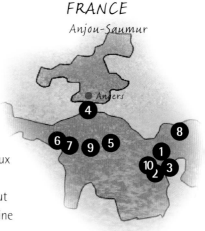

Chenin Blanc holds sway in Anjou-Saumur, producing whites in a range of styles. There are wonderfully dry whites from appellations like Savennières and Saumur. From the Coteaux du Layon, especially Bonnezeaux and the Quarts de Chaume, come some of the world's most delicious sweet wines. Less well known, the Côteaux de l'Aubance and Côteaux de Saumur also make some very good sweet wines. Saumur, with its many cellars cut into the limestone hillsides, is the center of sparkling wine production. And don't forget the area's rosés; watch for Cabernet de Saumur and Rosé de Loire.

The picturesque Château overlooks Saumur

1 Thierry Germain, Domaine des Roches Neuves, L'Insolite Saumur Blanc

The style of Thierry Germain's barrel-fermented, Insolite, made from old-vine Chenin Blanc, has evolved considerably over the past decade. Initially Insolite was rich, fat, and often high in alcohol, but Germain now searches for a more elegant, mineral-driven style. This change is apparent from 2006 onwards.

Food pairings: Broiled scallops
Vintage years: 2007, 2006

2 Domaine Saint-Just, Coulée Saint Cyr, Saumur Blanc

This barrel-fermented Chenin Blanc comes from Domaine de Saint-Just, run by Yves Lambert and his son Arnaud. The domaine was established by in 1996 and now has some 100 acres. The wine is rich and opulent, with just a touch of spice on the long finish.

Food pairings: Freshwater fish with beurre blanc
Vintage years: 2007, 2005

4 Domaine Richou, Chauvigné, Anjou Blanc

The Richou family have been installed in Anjou since the sixteenth century. Chauvigné is made from 100 percent Chenin Blanc. Vinified in stainless steel tanks, it spends a year on its lees to give it additional weight. Always very good value, Chauvigné has attractive peachy fruit and good minerality.

Food pairings: Salads
Vintage years: 2005

3 Château de Villeneuve, Saumur Blanc

The meticulous Jean-Pierre Chevallier has made this property one of the top producers in the Loire. This is his domaine white, made from 100 percent Chenin Blanc, of which the majority is fermented and aged in wood. The wine is quite rich, with apricot and honey flavors and a refreshing lemony finish.

Food pairings: Seafood risotto
Vintage years: 2006

5 Château de Fesles, Bonnezeaux ⓢⓦ

The Château de Fesles was bought by Bordeaux-born Bernard Germain in 1996, after the property had fallen into decline. As a result the wines are back on form. Its sweet Bonnezeaux shows both a mineral-driven intensity and precise balance of luscious sweetness and piercing acidity.

Food pairings: Blue cheeses
Vintage years: 2005 2003, 2001

6 Château d'Epiré, Savennières

Luc Brizard is a classic Savennières producer, and his estate is in the heart of this small appellation. His Savennières are often made in quite an austere style, so this wine needs several years of bottle age to show its best. It will also benefit from being decanted.

Food pairings: Oysters; broiled sea bass
Vintage years: 2006, 2005

7 Domaine du Closel, La Jalousie, Savennières

The Domaine du Closel is run by three generations of women from the de Jessey family. La Jalousie is a small valley planted with young vines, and this cuvée is their "entry level" Savennières. This is a mineral style of Savennières, with floral aromas when young.

Food pairings: Broiled or smoked fish
Vintage years: 2006, 2005, 2004

9 Baumard, Quarts de Chaume

The Quarts de Chaume, along with Bonnezeaux, are the two top microregions for making great sweet wines in the Layon Valley. This wine comes from a south-facing vineyard perfectly exposed to the mists arising from the Layon, which creates the ideal conditions for making botrytized wines.

Food pairings: Post-meal
Vintage years: 2006, 2005 2001

8 Domaine de Montgilet, Les Trois Schistes, Coteaux de l'Aubance

This estate is run by Victor and Vincent Lebreton. Les Trois Schistes is a blend from vineyards planted on three different types of schisteous soils. While this sweet wine is not super-concentrated, it has lovely apricot fruit balanced by clean acidity.

Food pairings: Rich pâtés, blue cheese, or alone as apéritif
Vintage years: 2005, 2002

10 Langlois-Chateau, Brut Rosé, Crémant de Loire

This producer has opted for the stricter *crémant de Loire* rules compared to those for sparkling Saumur. Made from 100 percent Cabernet Franc, this spends 18 months on its lees, which gives it a stream of fine bubbles. This pale pink crémant has attractive strawberry flavors.

Food pairings: Mild curries; tagines
Vintage years: NV

Grape picking season in the Loire Valley

Touraine

Touraine's best whites come from Vouvray and Montlouis and are made from Chenin Blanc in both sparkling and dry styles every year, while demi-sec and sweet wines are made only in good to great vintages. Wines from top producers can be very long-lived. Pétillant (semi-sparkling) wines from Vouvray and Montlouis are local specialties. Sauvignon (Blanc) de Touraine, especially from the Cher Valley, can be very good and is often very good value compared to the better-known Pouilly-Fumés and Sancerres. Also of note is the rare Cour-Cheverny made from the little-known Romorantin.

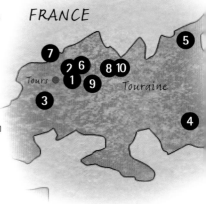

An old wine barrel used as a signpost, Loire Valley

1 Champalou, Cuvée des Fondreaux, Vouvray Sw

Founded in 1985 by Didier and Catherine Champalou, this family estate turns out an impeccable range of Vouvrays year after year. Cuvée des Fondreaux is their demi-sec cuvée, although the level of sweetness is not indicated on the bottle. The honeyed quince fruit is balanced by lemony acidity.

Food pairings: Chicken in cream sauce, pork and prunes
Vintage years: 2006, 2005

2 Domaine Huet, Le Mont Demi-Sec, Vouvray Sw 🛢

Demi-sec or medium-sweet is the traditional style of Vouvray, although Huet makes this style only when the vintage conditions permit. The additional sweetness of the demi-sec allows wines from good vintages to last for decades, becoming more honeyed as they age.

Food pairings: Rich pork dishes
Vintage years: 2006, 2005, 2002

4 Domaine Ricard, Le Petiot, Touraine Sauvignon

Based in the Cher Valley, Vincent Ricard is one of the best of the new generation of Touraine producers. Sauvignon Blanc is his specialty, and this is his most popular cuvée. It has an attractive weight and long-lasting grapefruit flavors.

Food pairings: Seafood platter; goat cheese
Vintage years: 2008

3 Clos Roche Blanche, Touraine Sauvignon

Catherine Roussel and Didier Barouillet of Clos Roche Blanche in the Cher Valley are organic producers of high-quality wines. This wine is usually fairly rich for a Touraine Sauvignon Blanc, thanks to its properly ripened fruit, but it has an attractive minerality. Keeps well for at least five years.

Food pairings: Goat cheese salad
Vintage years: 2007, 2006

5 Domaine des Huards, Cour-Cheverny 🛢

Cour-Cheverny is an appellation for wines made from the Romoratin grape, a rare variety with the capacity to age 10–20 years. The Gendriers' domaine is run organically. This wine can be lean and austere, although very pure, when young, but develops honeyed flavors with age.

Food pairings: Oysters; cream cheese
Vintage years: 2005, 2002

6 Domaine du Clos Naudin, Vouvray Sec

Along with Domaine Huet, Philippe Foreau's Domaine du Clos Naudin is one of the standard-bearers of Vouvray. The property makes sweet wines in the best years, but the dry cuvée is produced year in, year out—it's a luminous, mineral wine of great complexity.

Food pairings: Poached salmon
Vintage years: 2007, 2006, 2005

7 Domaine de Bellivière, Les Rosiers, Jasnières

Chenin Blanc is the only permitted grape variety in this small appelation. Eric Nicolas has been the area's leading producer since the 1990s. Les Rosiers comes from "young" vines (less than 50 years old!) and is a blend of ripe fruit and racy acidity.

Food pairings: Smoked salmon; salmon rillettes
Vintage years: 2006, 2005, 2004

9 François Chidaine Clos du Breuil, Montlouis

François Chidaine, who owns vines in Vouvray, Montlouis, and the Cher Valley, has been biodynamic since 1999. Chidaine loves his wines to be mineral and pure, and the Clos du Breuil is no exception. Virtually bone-dry in most vintages, it's a little richer in hot years like 2005 and 2003.

Food pairings: Broiled fish
Vintage years: 2007, 2006, 2005

8 Jacky Blot, Domaine de la Taille aux Loups, Triple Zero, Montlouis Pétillant

Jacky Blot makes brilliant semi-sparkling non-vintage wine from ripe Chenin Blanc with no sugar added at any stage of the process, hence the name. This cuvée has gentle, persistent lemony flavors with some toasted brioche notes.

Food pairings: Broiled shrimp
Vintage years: NV

10 Château Aulée, Crémant de Loire

This elegant château near Azay-le-Rideau was built in 1856 by Bordeaux négociant Cordier, and is now owned by Arnaud and Marielle Henrion. Made in a similar way to Champagne, this lively, creamy sparkler is made from Chenin Blanc.

Food pairings: Shellfish; alone as apéritif
Vintage years: NV

Sparkling wine bottles in *pupitres*, Vouvray

Upper Loire

This is very much fashionable Sauvignon Blanc country, with Sancerre and Pouilly-Fumé the two main appellations. Crisp, aromatic wines are made here from the Sauvignon Blanc grapes, as well as in the smaller appellations of Menetou-Salon, Quincy, Reuilly and the Coteaux de Giennois. The climate here is semi-continental and the majority of the vineyards are planted on limestone. Many of these wines are made to drink young, although the best will age and develop greater complexity. Chasselas is the only other white variety grown here, and only in the appellation of Pouilly-sur-Loire, where production is tiny.

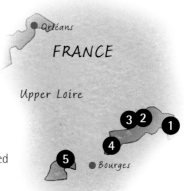

Sauvignon Blanc grapes on the vine

1 Didier Dagueneau, Blanc Fumé de Pouilly, Silex, Pouilly-Fumé

The late Didier Dagueneau was the producer of one of the world's greatest dry Sauvignon Blancs, Silex. It comes from a very flinty vineyard, hence its name. Vinified in barriques, this complex and ageworthy wine varies in weight from year to year, but always has great citric minerality and precision.

Food pairings: Top-quality fish or shellfish, either broiled or sauteéd
Vintage years: 2007, 2006, 2005

2 Lucien Crochet, Sancerre Pinot Rosé Loire, Central Vineyards, Sancerre ®

All too often Sancerre Rosé is disappointing and overpriced, but this well-made rosé is an exception. It has real character, juicy red fruit flavors, as well as weight and length. This rosé is bottled every May, so look for the latest vintage.

Food pairings: Light lunches; mildly spiced Asian dishes
Vintage years: 2008

4 Domaine Henry Pellé, Morogues, Menetou-Salon

Morogues is one of the main communes in the appellation of Menetou-Salon and Domaine Henry Pellé is a leading producer. The wines here are often a little less racy than those of Sancerre. This has attractive gooseberry fruit and is best drunk within three years of vintage.

Food pairings: Shrimp salad
Vintage years: 2008, 2007

3 Alphonse Mellot, La Moussière, Sancerre

This top-quality domaine was established in 1513 and has been run by Alphonse Mellot ever since. La Moussière comes from a well-exposed vineyard to the west of the town of Sancerre. Half the cuvée is fermented in stainless steel and the other half in oak, giving it rich grapefruit flavors.

Food pairings: Broiled salmon
Vintage years: 2007, 2006, 2005

5 Jean Tatin, Quincy

Quincy is a small appellation that makes whites from Sauvignon Blanc planted on gravel terraces. Vinified in stainless steel, this cuvée has classic gooseberry and grapefruit flavors and a refreshing citric finish. Often quite lean when released, it tends to take on more weight with a few months in bottle.

Food pairings: Quiche, fishcakes
Vintage years: 2007, 2006, 2005

1 2 3 4 5

Bordeaux, dry whites

Bordeaux is famed for its iconic reds, which makes it easy to forget that it produces whites and rosés too. In particular, the châteaux of Pessac-Léognan in the Graves are celebrated for their rich, long-lived dry whites. The main grapes used in dry wines are Sauvignon Blanc and Sémillon, but sometimes a little Muscadelle or Sauvignon Gris is added to the blend.

Muscadelle grapes, Château Bonnet, Entre-Deux-Mers

1 Château Brown, Blanc, Pessac-Léognan

Much money has been invested in Château Brown since it was bought by the Mau family in 2004, and it's beginning to show in the rapidly improving quality of its wines. The white is rich in aromatic Sauvignon Blanc, but up to 40 percent of Sémillon lends weight to the blend.

Food pairings: Firm white fish
Vintage years: 2007, 2005, 2004

2 Domaine de Chevalier, Blanc, Grand Cru Classé de Graves, Pessac-Léognan

You may have to take out a second mortgage in order to buy a bottle of Domaine de Chevalier, but you probably won't regret it. This blend of 70 percent Sauvignon Blanc and 30 percent Sémillon is fermented in oak barrels to give it extra richness and weight.

Food pairings: Roast pork or chicken; firm-fleshed white fish
Vintage years: 2007, 2005, 2004

4 Vieux Château Gaubert, Blanc, Graves

A roughly equal blend of Sémillon and Sauvignon Blanc, the restrained, sophisticated white wine made at Vieux Château Gaubert punches way above its weight when compared to some of the bigger names in the region. It will repay a couple of years' aging in bottle.

Food pairings: Skate with beurre noir
Vintage years: 2007, 2005, 2004

3 Clos Floridène, Blanc, Graves

Clos Floridène is owned by Denis Dubourdieu, a respected oenological consultant. He brings all his expertise to bear on his own wine, a delicious—and reasonably priced—barrel-fermented wine that is delightful when drunk young but can age well for up to a decade.

Food pairings: Firm white fish
Vintage years: 2007, 2005, 2004

5 Pavillon Blanc de Château Margaux, Bordeaux

Château Margaux is, of course, one of the five first growth châteaux of the region, so it's surprising to discover that its white wine is labeled as "mere" Bordeaux. Nevertheless, this is still an outstanding wine whose intensity and concentration allows it to age with incredible finesse.

Food pairings: White fish; chicken
Vintage years: 2007, 2005, 2001

 1 2 3 4 5

6 Château Haut-Bailly, Rosé, Bordeaux

Château Haut-Bailly may be located in Pessac-Léognan, but unlike many of its neighbors, it focuses on producing red wines rather than whites. Its rosé is a bit of a gem, much appreciated by aficionados around the world for its delicate rose- and strawberry-scented palate.

Food pairings: Lightly spiced curries; summer salads
Vintage years: 2008

7 Château Carbonnieux, Blanc, Pessac-Léognan

While not the most adventurous producer in the Graves, Château Carbonnieux is widely regarded as being a safe pair of hands in terms of the production of white wines. Fermented in barrel, this is a rich, creamy wine with a good, solid pedigree.

Food pairings: Roast chicken
Vintage years: 2007, 2005, 2004

9 Château Bonnet, Blanc, Entre-Deux-Mers

The Lurton family, who own Château Bonnet, may well be Bordeaux royalty, but that doesn't mean that they're not prepared to make sensibly priced wines for everyday drinking. This white is not meant for long aging, but is nevertheless both fresh and pleasant, with a bracing citrus palate.

Food pairings: Seafood
Vintage years: 2008, 2007

8 Château Smith-Haut-Lafitte, Blanc, Pessac-Léognan

Although 80 percent of Smith-Haut-Lafitte's production is focused on red wine, the château makes a very fine white. Sauvignon Blanc is the main component in the blend, with slightly less Sémillon plus a splash of the rare Sauvignon Gris. Its floral, herbal flavors are given weight by rich oak.

Food pairings: Sushi; white fish
Vintage years: 2007, 2005, 2001

10 Château de Giscours, Le Rosé de Giscours, Bordeaux

Château de Giscours, located in the commune of Margaux, receives much acclaim for its polished, elegant red wines. Few people know that it also makes a rosé, which is a shame as this is a wonderfully refreshing, strawberry-scented wine. Perfect for a summer's evening.

Food pairings: Charcuterie
Vintage years: 2008

Château-Smith-Haut-Lafitte and vineyards, Pessac-Léognan

Bordeaux, sweet whites

The appellations that hug the shores of the Garonne and Ciron Rivers, of which Sauternes is the most renowned, are famed for their sweet white wines. The main grapes used in sweet wines are Sauvignon Blanc and Sémillon, but sometimes a little Muscadelle or Sauvignon Gris is added to the blend.

The well-tended vineyards of Château d'Yquem, Sauternes, Bordeaux

❶ Château Bastor-Lamontagne, Sauternes Ⓢ

The wines of Sauternes don't tend to come cheap, but Bastor-Lamontagne consistently manages to deliver value for money compared to some of its more expensive neighbors (such as Château Suduiraut, just a short distance to the south). A luscious, honeyed blend of Sémillon, Sauvignon Blanc, and Muscadelle.

Food pairings: Crème brûlée
Vintage years: 2007, 2005, 2001

❷ Château La Rame, Sainte-Croix-du-Mont Ⓢ

Situated on the right bank of the Garonne, Château La Rame consistently produces balanced sweet wines that are far more affordable than those from more prestigious appellations. This basic cuvée is made in a light, fresh style, but if you want something more potent, try the Réserve du Château.

Food pairings: Apricot tart; tarte tatin
Vintage years: 2007, 2005, 2001

❹ Château d'Yquem, 1er Grand Cru Classé, Sauternes Ⓢ 🛢

For many, Château d'Yquem is the *ne plus ultra* of sweet wines. Its pleasures come at a cost, but bear in mind the fact that the château only produces a single glass of wine per vine—and then only in the very best years.

Food pairings: Savor each sip by itself
Vintage years: 2007, 2005, 2001

❸ Château Suduiraut, 1er Cru Classé, Sauternes Ⓢ 🛢

Long-lived and potent, with flavors tinged with honey and saffron, Suduiraut is widely considered to be second in quality only to the world-famous Yquem. Despite all the richness, Suduiraut's wine always shows exemplary balance and precision. At its best with a bit of bottle age.

Food pairings: Rich egg custards; pineapple tarte tatin
Vintage years: 2007, 2005, 2001

❺ Château Climens, 1er Cru Classé, Barsac Ⓢ

Although most of Bordeaux's sweet wines are based on a blend of Sémillon and Sauvignon Blanc, Climens is made exclusively from Sémillon. This means they often show less tropical fruit than many of the region's sweet wines, but they compensate with zesty citrus flavors and a toasted nuttiness.

Food pairings: Tarte au citron
Vintage years: 2007, 2006, 2005

The Dordogne

The Dordogne is probably more famed for its holiday cottages than for its wines. It's a shame when you consider that this area, which lies on the northeastern fringes of Bordeaux, can give its more famous neighbor a run for its money when it comes to both dry and sweet whites, as well as rosés. Both soils and climate are similar to those prevailing on Bordeaux's Right Bank. What's more, you'll find pretty much the same grape varieties grown in both regions. If you add it all up, Bergerac's wines offer a terrific bargain for the savvy wine lover.

Vineyard bathed in sunlight in the Bergerac region

① Château Tour des Gendres, Moulin des Dames Blanc, Bergerac

Luc de Conti is widely credited with being the driving force behind the revitalization of the Bergerac appellation. Both his whites and his reds show incredible finesse and a real sense of place. The Moulin des Dames is rich and creamy, but is also incredibly well balanced and complex.

Food pairings: White fish, roast pork with apricots
Vintage years: 2006, 2005, 2004

② Château Laulerie, Rosé, Bergerac ®

The Dubard family have made quite a reputation for the quality of their delightfully refreshing rosé. A classic Bordeaux blend of Cabernet Sauvignon, Cabernet Franc, Merlot, and Malbec, this sunset-pink wine has enough density of red berry-flavored fruit to make it a very versatile food wine.

Food pairings: Seared tuna
Vintage years: 2008

④ Château Tirecul-la-Gravière, Monbazillac Sw

Like the sweet wines of Sauternes, those of Monbazillac depend on grapes becoming infected with botrytis. The result is the same luscious, honeyed sweetness, which, in the case of this wine is balanced with enough acidity to prevent the wine from becoming cloying.

Food pairings: Crème brûlée or crème caramel
Vintage years: 2004, 2003, 2001

③ Domaine de l'Ancienne Cure, Bergerac Sec

The Domaine de l'Ancienne Cure is best known for its sweet wines, but its dry white, a blend of 70 percent Sauvignon Blanc and 30 percent Sémillon, is a long-standing personal favorite. It has a creamy texture, thanks to time spent on lees, but its hallmark is its fresh, zingy acidity.

Food pairings: Smoked fish; salads
Vintage years: 2008, 2007, 2005

⑤ Clos d'Yvigne, Saussignac Sw

Patricia Atkinson has beaten all kinds of odds in order to make wine in the Dordogne. She's even written a fascinating book about her struggle to survive and thrive. Atkinson has succeeded admirably—and this marvelous sweet wine is the absolute proof of just how well she's doing.

Food pairings: Tarte tatin, sticky toffee pudding, pecan pie
Vintage years: 2007, 2005, 2001

Southwest

Southwest France is a loose, catchall term for a vast sweep of territory that runs up the Atlantic coast, from the Basque territories clustered around the Spanish border to the fringes of Bordeaux, and stretching as far east as Toulouse, Albi, and Cahors. Its wines are sweet, dry, sparkling—and pretty much everything in between—and there are rosés aplenty too. A plethora of quirky grape varieties are planted in the area in addition to well-known crowd-pleasers. In short, the region offers something to please pretty much every palate and every wallet.

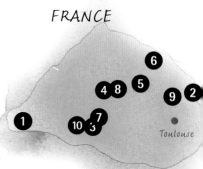

FRANCE

Toulouse

Vineyards among farmland near Cahors

1 Domaine Arretxea, Hegoxuri, Irouléguy

Hidden away in the mountainous Basque country, the appellation of Irouléguy produces some wild and wonderful whites. The most wonderful of them all, a sumptuously rich blend of Petit Manseng, Gros Manseng, and Petit Courbu, is produced by the Riouspeyous family, who run their vineyards along biodynamic principles.

Food pairings: Sushi; Thai dishes
Vintage years: 2007, 2006

2 Domaine les Tres Cantous, Mauzac Nature, Vin de Table de France ⑤

Robert Plageolles is the king of Mauzac, a local grape variety. This particular cuvée is a low-alcohol sparkler that tastes of green apples. His Mauzac wines run the gamut from dry and crisp to lusciously sweet.

Food pairings: Apéritif
Vintage years: NV

4 Alain Brumont, Jardins de Bouscassé, Pacherenc du Vic-Bilh Sec

Southwest France is full of wine-makers with big personalities, but Alain Brumont bestrides the area like a colossus. Known best for his Madirans, he also makes delicious, vibrant whites. This is a lively wine with loads of zingy apricot fruit.

Food pairings: Chinese stir-fries
Vintage years: 2007, 2006, 2005

3 Clos Lapeyre, Vitatge Vielh, Jurançon

"Vitatge Vielh" means "old vines" in the local dialect, and Jean-Bernard Larrieu's 3.5-acre parcel of vines averages around 60 years, which gives the wine a certain power and concentration. It gets its tropical fruit aromas from its blend of Petit and Gros Manseng, plus a touch of Petit Courbu.

Food pairings: Rich pâtés; mildly spiced dishes
Vintage years: 2005, 2004

5 Domaine Tariquet, Ugni Blanc Colombard, Vin de Pays des Côtes de Gascogne

Domaine Tariquet specializes in the production of Armagnac brandy, but it also makes a fine range of easy-drinking everyday wines. This blend is based on two of the region's workhorse grapes, but that's not to denigrate its fresh, grassy, easy-drinking appeal.

Food pairings: Steamed fish
Vintage years: 2008

6 Domaine d'Escausses, La Vigne de l'Oubli, Blanc, Gaillac

The grapes for La Vigne de l'Oubli come from 15- to 50-year-old vines of Sauvignon Blanc, Mauzac, and Muscadelle. After it has been aged on its lees in new oak, Denis Ballaran's white blend combines both a creamy texture and subtly spiced aromas of dried fruits and fresh apples.

2006
la Vigne de l'oubli
domaine d'Escausses
APPELLATION GAILLAC CONTRÔLÉE

Food pairings: Creamy curries; sushi
Vintage years: 2006, 2005

7 Didier Dagueneau, Les Jardins de Babylone, Jurançon

The late Dagueneau was best known for his cult wines from the Loire, but also started making sweet wines in Jurançon. Dagueneau's premature death has made prices rocket, but these are truly sublime wines and aficionados would argue they're worth every penny.

Food pairings: Foie gras; blue cheese
Vintage years: 2006, 2005, 2004

9 Château de Plaisance, Rosé, Côtes du Frontonnais ®

This pretty sunset-pink wine is a blend of 65 percent Négrette (a local grape variety), 15 percent Syrah, and 20 percent Gamay. But who cares about statistics when you can just kick back and enjoy a wine that offers such punchy, peppery intensity?

Food pairings: Charcuterie platters; seared tuna or salmon
Vintage years: 2008

8 Domaine Berthoumieu, Symphonie d'Automne, Pacherenc du Vic-Bilh Doux

Didier Barré is best known for his hefty Madirans, but he also makes a couple of whites. This is made from grapes harvested in three passes through the vineyards, thus ensuring perfect ripeness. A wine made to be sipped and savored slowly.

Food pairings: Rich patés
Vintage years: 2007, 2006, 2005

10 Domaine Cauhapé, Symphonie de Novembre, Jurançon

Domaine Cauhapé's wines are the most highly prized Jurançons in the world. Most sweet cuvées are named for their time of harvest. The later the harvest, the sweeter the wine, and this perfumed, spicy wine lies somewhere in the middle of the scale.

Food pairings: Foie gras, sheep's cheeses, sweet nutty desserts
Vintage years: 2005, 2003

A pail laden with Gros and Petit Manseng grapes destined to make Jurnaçon

Languedoc & Roussillon

FRANCE

It's impossible to generalize about the wines produced in Languedoc and Roussillon. Thanks to variations in climate, which ranges from Mediterranean warmth near the sea to near-continental coolness up in the inland hills, and a huge diversity of soil types, the region's winemakers are free to create virtually any style of wine they want. Fortified sweet wines used to be a key style, but nowadays you'll find dry whites that range from fresh and zesty to concentrated and powerful, as well as rosés and sparkling crémants. No wonder so many young, dynamic winemakers have been attracted to the region in recent years.

Vineyards near the foothills of the Pyrenées, Roussillon

1 Olivier Pithon, La D-18, Vin de Pays des Côtes Catalanes

Olivier Pithon is an iconoclastic Che Guevara look-alike who has named his top white cuvée after the road that runs through his vineyard. A blend of Grenaches Blanc and Gris, this extraordinary aromatic wine repays decanting when young, but is even better when aged a bit in bottle.

Food pairings: Roast monkfish; pancetta
Vintage years: 2006, 2004, 2002

2 Domaine Mas Amiel, Vintage Blanc, Maury ⓢⓦ

Mas Amiel, whose vineyards are located on the schisteous slopes of Maury, is best known for its fortified red Grenaches—a very traditional style of wine in these parts. This wine, made from Grenache Gris, is also fortified to create a rich sweet wine with spicy pear and citrus notes.

Food pairings: Lobster salad with citrus-ginger dressing
Vintage years: 1999, 1998, 1996

4 Domaine des Schistes, Solera, Rivesaltes ⓢⓦ

Rivesaltes has specialized for generations in fortified Muscats. Some are aged in a solera, meaning that each bottling is a blend of vintages, ensuring not only consistency of style, but also complexity. This wine is full of smoky, dried fruit flavors.

Food pairings: Blue cheese; apricot and almond tart
Vintage years: NV

3 Domaine Gauby, Vielles Vignes Blanc, Vin de Pays des Côtes Catalanes

Gérard Gauby was growing grapes in Roussillon long before it became a fashionable enclave. His Vielles Vignes packs an aromatic punch, thanks to its 50- to 100-year-old vines and complex blend. The wine is part-aged in oak, adding further richness.

Food pairings: Roast pork with fennel and garlic
Vintage years: 2006, 2005, 2004

5 Préceptorie de Centernach, Rosé, Côtes du Roussillon Ⓡ

Maury's Préceptorie de Centernach, is owned by the Parcé brothers who also own the Domaine de la Rectorie in Banyuls. Famed for their sweet wines, their dry wines are also noteworthy. This is a Grenache-based pink that deserves to be matched with equally weighty food.

Food pairings: Mild lamb curry
Vintage years: 2008

1  2 3 4 5

6 Mas de Daumas Gassac, Blanc, Vin de Pays de l'Hérault

Probably the most famous wine-growing property in this part of the world, Mas de Daumas Gassac eschews the appellation system in favor of the flexibility of making Vins de Pays. A complex harmony of various grape varieties, this wine should not be served too cold. Decanting wouldn't hurt either.

Food pairings: Rich seafood dishes, chicken in a creamy sauce
Vintage years: 2007, 2006, 2005

7 Domaine Félines Jourdan, Picpoul de Pinet

Southern France's equivalent of Muscadet, the wines made from the Picpoul de Pinet grape have a saline tang that underpins their citrus fruit. Could it be because the vineyards lie near the seashore? No one really knows, but all are unanimous in acknowledging that this is an ideal wine for seafood.

Food pairings: Oysters; shellfish
Vintage years: 2008

9 Domaine de Barroubio, Muscat de St. Jean de Minervois ⓢ

Domaine de Barroubio's vineyards are located on the chalky plateau of St. Jean de Minervois. The area is famed for its sweet fortified Muscats, and Barroubio is one of its top producers. This version is fresh and floral, with the perfect balance of sugar and zesty acidity.

Food pairings: Fruity desserts
Vintage years: 2008

8 Domaine Clavel, Mescladis, Rosé, Coteaux du Languedoc ⓡ

Rosé wines have long been part of southern France's wine-making tradition, so no wonder they get it right so often. Domaine Clavel's Mescladis is made mainly from Syrah, with a dollop of Cinsault thrown in. It tastes of ripe, tangy red currants.

Food pairings: Picnics, feta and watermelon salad, salade niçoise
Vintage years: 2008

10 Domaine Mouscaillo, Chardonnay, Limoux

The hills that surround the town of Limoux are noted as a source of elegant, fresh Chardonnay wines, thanks to their cool climate. Mouscaillo's wines are among the best, showing pure fruit and some minerality, along with a creamy texture derived from aging in large oak barrels.

Food pairings: Roast chicken, firm-fleshed white fish
Vintage years: 2006, 2005

Off the beaten track, vineyards at Cazedarnes, Hérault

Rhône

There are two distinct personalities to the River Rhône. In the north it is a rushing, cutting river, forging its way between the rocky hillsides, overlooked by vineyards that cling to the slopes. In the south, it broadens outs, slows down, and meanders through the countryside, giving its name to a vast productive landscape.

Most people think of the Rhône as being a region for red wines. While it's true that most of the vineyards that line the river are planted with red grapes, there are some very fine white wines made in the area, including Condrieu, the appellation that sets the benchmark for Viognier around the world. Marsanne and Roussanne also thrive in the region's continental north, and are often part of the blend in the warmer southern area. The Southern Rhône is also a great source of powerful, richly flavored rosés, while producers in both the north and the south make some wonderful sweet wines.

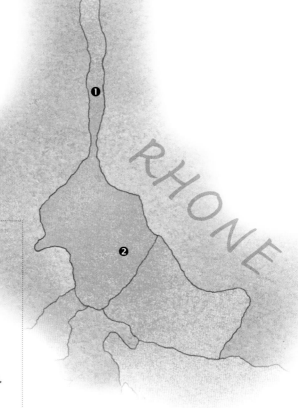

❶ Northern Rhône

❷ Southern Rhône

RHONE

The climate in Rhône is
renowned for being really
variable. If summers are
hot, they stay quite humid,
winters are then quite
cold due to the presence
of mountains. The region
benefits from 1,976 sunshine
hours a year.

Northern Rhône

The continental climate of the Northern Rhône, with its hot summer days and cold winters, makes it a great place to grow Syrah, a red grape. But let's not forget that the region is also home to some very fine white wines, including Condrieu, the appellation that sets the benchmark for lush, apricot-scented Viognier around the world. Opulent, nutty Marsanne and racy, floral Roussanne also thrive on the steep terraces that line the river, and can be vinified separately or blended together. Dessert wines made in the region from late-harvest or even raisined Viognier grapes are a particular treat.

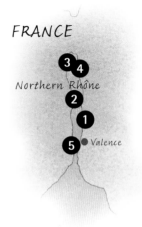

FRANCE

Northern Rhône

Valence

Wines made in the commune of Condrieu are exclusively white

1 Michel Chapoutier, Chante Alouette, Hermitage Blanc

Chapoutier is one of the biggest names in the Northern Rhône, and the wines of Hermitage are his specialty. Chante Alouette, which is made from Marsanne, is the "entry level" cuvée, a rich, honeyed, quince- and almond-scented wine that is surprisingly long-lived.

Food pairings: Broiled, buttered lobster; mildly spiced Asian dishes
Vintage years: 2006, 2005

2 Domaine Yves Cuilleron, Le Lombard, St. Joseph Blanc

The dashing Yves Cuilleron is one of the young turks of the Northern Rhône. Rather unusually, he's better known for his white wines than his reds, particularly his Condrieus and his St. Josephs. The powerful but restrained Lombard is based on 40-year-old Marsanne vines.

Food pairings: Fish in beurre blanc sauce
Vintage years: 2007, 2006

4 Domaine René Rostaing, La Bonnette, Condrieu

René Rostaing is one of the best producers of reds in Côte-Rôtie. His Condrieu, on the other hand, is more of a quiet success story. With its sumptuous peach and passion fruit flavors, and a streak of minerality, this is a wine to enjoy in the flower of its youth.

Food pairings: Broiled lobster with butter sauce
Vintage years: 2008, 2007

3 Domaine Pierre Gaillard, Fleurs d'Automne, Vendange Tardive, Condrieu ⓢⓦ

A handful of producers make late harvest (vendange tardive) or raisined versions of Condrieu. Gaillard's version is lusciously sweet and perfumed, yet stops itself from tipping over into an excess of sugar.

Food pairings: Broiled peaches with caramelized butter
Vintage years: 2007, 2006

5 Domaine du Tunnel, Cuvée Roussanne, Saint-Péray

Saint-Péray is normally the place to look for sparkling wines, although not much of the stuff ever leaves France. The Domaine du Tunnel is unusual in that they make a still wine from the nervy, fine-boned Roussanne grape. There's also a richer, more concentrated Préstige cuvée.

Food pairings: Thai seafood salad
Vintage years: 2007, 2006

1 𝄃𝄃𝄃𝄃𝄃 2 𝄃𝄃𝄃 3 𝄃𝄃𝄃𝄃𝄃 4 𝄃𝄃𝄃𝄃𝄃 5 𝄃𝄃𝄃

Southern Rhône

By the time you reach the broad delta of the Rhône, the climate has shifted from cool continental to warm Mediterranean. There is little rain in the region, and the grapes that thrive here need to be able to cope with drought conditions. Winemakers often hedge their bets by planting a variety of grapes, so the Southern Rhône is a region of blends. Grapes include Grenache Blanc, Roussanne, Marsanne, Bourboulenc, Clairette, and Viognier. Look out, as well, for the sweet fortified Muscats produced in the appellation of Beaumes-de-Venise—and don't forget the punchy rosés produced in the region.

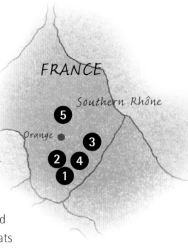

Châteauneuf-du-Pape translates as "New Castle of the Pope"—the history of this commune and its wine is firmly entwined with papal history

1 Domaine de la Mordorée, Rosé, Tavel ®

Tavel is an appellation dedicated to the production of rosé wines. Domaine de la Mordorée's version, sometimes labeled as "La Dame Rousse," is a particularly good example of this deep pink wine. It has more density of fruit than most rosés, and really needs food to perform at its best.

Food pairings: Grilled meats, broiled lamb with herbs and garlic
Vintage years: 2008, 2007

2 Domaine Maby, La Fermade, Blanc, Lirac

Domaine Maby's typical Southern Rhône blend of Grenache Blanc, Picpoul, and Clairette is not a wine that's meant to be taken too seriously or aged for too long. Instead, enjoy it young for its fruity palate and crisp acidity. Great value for money.

Food pairings: Firm-fleshed white fish
Vintage years: 2008, 2007

4 Domaine de Marcoux, Blanc, Châteauneuf-du-Pape

This domaine was one of the pioneers of biodynamics in the Rhône, and this wine is a delicious, complex wine of great depth. This quality is a result of the interplay of viticultural philosophy and a talented winemaker.

Food pairings: Pork with fennel and garlic, braised rabbit
Vintage years: 2007, 2005, 2004

3 Domaine de Durban, Muscat de Beaumes de Venise Ⓢⓦ

The fortified Muscats of Beaumes de Venise were at their height of popularity in the 1970s–1980s and are just about due to be re-discovered. Better balanced than many, this is a sweet wine that tastes of honeyed grapes, ripe peaches, and white flowers.

Food pairings: Poached peaches, blue cheese, fruit tarts

5 Domaine Daniel et Denis Alary, La Font d'Estevenas Blanc, Cairanne

Cairanne is one of the named villages of the area, so its wines should be a notch above the run of the mill. Father and son team Daniel and Denis Alary make a a rich blend of Roussanne, Marsanne, Viognier, and Clairette.

Food pairings: Scallops, mildly spiced Asian dishes, roast pork

Provence

Provence is best known for its beaches. Its wines are seldom taken seriously, partly because the area's traditional specialty is rosé—a style wine snobs have difficulty taking seriously. However, as more and more of us have taken to drinking pink wine in recent years, Provence is starting to benefit from the growing interest. In addition to rosés, the area also makes some startlingly good reds and whites, all of which are based on the same grapes grown around France's Mediterranean coastline. The island of Corsica, which lies off the Mediterranean coast, is another source of stunning rosés and whites.

Moonlit vineyards near Les Baux, Provence

1 Château de Pibarnon, Rosé, Bandol ®

The appellation of Bandol is highly prized for its rosé wines, and the Château de Pibarnon is one of its foremost producers. Its rosé is a beautiful pale salmon pink, the traditional hue of Provencal rosés—a color that in no way indicates lack of concentration or fruit.

Food pairings: Broiled salmon or tuna, salade niçoise
Vintage years: 2008

2 Domaine de Trévallon, Blanc, Vin de Pays des Bouches du Rhône

Eloi Dürrbach makes some of Provence's most acclaimed wines, yet due to a quirk in the appellation system they are classified as Vins de Pays. Whatever label you stick on this barrel-fermented blend of Marsanne, Roussanne, and Chardonnay, it's a fine wine.

Food pairings: Herb-stuffed sea bass; monkfish
Vintage years: 2007, 2005

4 Commanderie de Peyrassol, Rosé, Côtes de Provence ®

The Commanderie de Peyrassol, which was founded in the thirteenth century, is noted for its permanent art collection and its fresh, zesty rosé. A traditional blend of Grenache Noir, Cinsault, and Syrah, this has more concentration and depth than most Provençal pinks.

Food pairings: Broiled salmon
Vintage years: 2008

3 Clos Poggiale, Vermentino, Corsica

Robert Skalli, who owns Corsica's Clos Poggiale, is a larger-than-life character, and this is reflected in the broad, sweeping palate of this potent wine. Citrus fruits dominate both the nose and palate, but there's an underlying minerality giving it an edge of sophistication.

Food pairings: Broiled fish, goat or sheep's cheese
Vintage years: 2007

5 Domaine de la Suffrène, Rosé, Bandol ®

Cédric Gravier left his local cooperative at the end of the 1990s to strike out on his own. He's become a bit of a local star in the intervening decade, and his rosé, a blend of Mourvèdre, Grenache, Cinsault, and Carignan, is an absolute delight of a summer wine.

Food pairings: Bouillabaise or other fish stews
Vintage years: 2008

Italy

The ancient Greeks called Italy "Oenotria"—the land of wine—for good reason: both red and white wines are produced from the northern tip to the southern toe of the country and from a mind-boggling array of grapes. Many Italian regions offer the perfect combination of sun-drenched slopes, temperate climate, and ideal soils for vine growing. The country's wine production is huge; indeed Italy is the largest producer in the world in many vintages or the second behind France.

Of course, big isn't necessarily beautiful. Today, Italy's greatest challenge is to adapt to lower consumption patterns by reducing yields, uprooting poor vineyards, and focusing more attention on the middle- to upper-quality tiers. Good progress has already been made, especially for white wines. Importantly, winemakers have learned how to achieve local character in their wines through a combination of better viticulture and a light touch in the winery.

This trend is not necessarily new in the north, but there have been eyebrow-raising changes in the south in recent years. Who could have predicted the seismic change in Sicily that has brought both exciting and very affordable wines to the table?

Italy offers a colorful array of white wines—dry, sweet, and sparkling—made from a choice of grapes ranging from Arneis to Zibibbo as well as an inspiring cuisine to accompany them. If the choice looks a bit daunting, a good wine merchant will guide you through the treasure trove.

Northwest Italy

Piedmont, bordered by the Alps, is home to some of Italy's most distinctive white and sparkling wines, though they are often eclipsed by the famous reds made from the Nebbiolo grape. The area's subalpine climate is ideal for the production of aromatic grapes, including Moscato (Muscat), Arneis, and Cortese. The wines tend to be delicate and light, and oak is rarely used. The Valle d'Aosta owes much of its winemaking tradition—and its grapes—to French and Swiss influences. Although the wines can be difficult to track down, persevere for the sake of their delicate, floral aromatics.

Stainless steel tanks, Braida Winery, Piedmont

① Antonio Deltetto, San Michele, Roero Arneis

The grapes for this wine are sourced from the 30-year-old San Michele vineyard in the gentle hilly region on the northern bank of the River Tanaro. A soft, well-balanced wine, thanks to some of the must being barrel-fermented. Crisp apple and pear fruit with good length.

Food pairings: Baked trout
Vintage years: 2008, 2007

② Marco Porello, Camestri, Roero Arneis

Arneis is one of Piedmont's indigenous white grape varieties, and evidence suggests that it has been cultivated in the province for at least the past four centuries. Marco Porello's take on the grape is crisp and refreshing, with brisk, mineral-tinged orchard and citrus fruit and a pleasant length.

Food pairings: Roast sea bass stuffed with herbs
Vintage years: 2008, 2007

④ Les Crêtes, Chardonnay, Cuvée Frissonière, Valle d'Aosta

If the name of this wine sounds French, it's because the Aosta Valley straddles the Alps along the Italian–French border, so Gallic influence is strong. Chardonnay is commonly grown in the valley, and this cuvée is full of crisp pear and apple fruit.

Food pairings: Antipasto; prosciutto
Vintage years: 2006, 2004, 2001

③ Braida, Vigna Senza Nome, Moscato d'Asti

This sweet wine is typical of the Muscat-based wines made in the vineyards around the Piedmontese town of Asti. Gently sparkling and low in alcohol, it tastes of freshly squeezed grapes, with hints of rose petals and orange blossoms. Enjoy it young, before it loses all its *joie de vivre*.

Food pairings: Fresh strawberries, hazelnut cake
Vintage years: 2008

⑤ La Giustiniana, Vigneti Lugarara, Gavi

Cortese grapes can produce spectacular wines given careful attention in the vineyard and by the winemaker, as this wine shows. La Giustiniana is given cool fermentation and bottled the spring after harvest when it reveals fresh but rich citrus flavors. A vibrant, unoaked wine.

Food pairings: Seafood pasta; baked or broiled fish
Vintage years: 2008, 2007

Northeast Italy

The Veneto, home to Soave, some of the best Pinot Grigio wines, and the increasingly popular Prosecco sparkling wines, is northeast Italy's central hub for white wine. However, Alto-Adige, to the north, adds rich diversity, thanks to its Austrian heritage and vineyards that reach dizzying heights. Other areas of note include Friuli-Venezia-Giulia, which borders Slovenia in the east. Friuli's impressively dry, elegant, and perfumed wines, made predominantly by family-run producers, have won well-deserved international acclaim in recent decades.

Prosecco vines growing in Guia, Veneto

1 Pieropan, Soave Classico, La Rocca, Soave

In the context of Soave, Leonildo Pieropan is a name to be reckoned with. La Rocca is his top cuvée, made from late-harvested Garganega grapes and aged in oak for a year. It has richness and weight, and a palate redolent with honeyed almond flavors.

Food pairings: Poached salmon; dressed crab
Vintage years: 2006, 2005, 2002

2 Cavit, Bottega Vinai Pinot Grigio, Trentino

Pinot Grigio grows throughout northeast Italy, but gives its best performance on the vineyard slopes of the cooler Trentino region. This more traditional style has attractive floral intensity, with delicate lemon and lychee flavors on the palate in a structured style that will develop gracefully over a year.

Food pairings: Chicken salad
Vintage years: 2008, 2007

4 Cantina Terlano Gewürztraminer, Alto Adige

Aromatic grape varieties thrive on the remarkably steep slopes of this northern Italian region. The purity of fruit shines through in this unoaked wine, supported by mineral freshness. Elegant yet powerful with high alcohol by Italy's standards—Alto Adige's whites are strictly for food.

Food pairings: Asparagus risotto
Vintage years: 2008, 2007

3 Inama, Soave Classico, Soave

Inama makes three levels of Soave, beginning with this unoaked version. Made from 30-year-old Garganega vines, it is an intense wine of great purity, with aromas of sun-warmed stones and lemon zest, and a hint of almonds on the finish. Terrific value for money.

Food pairings: Salads; Dover sole
Vintage years: 2007, 2006

5 Bisol, Crede, Prosecco di Valdobbiadene Brut

Bisol is one of the foremost producers of sparkling wines in the Prosecco area. The name of this cuvée refers to the clay and sandstone soil of the vineyards where the grapes are grown. It's an intense wine, with honeyed notes of apples and pears.

Food pairings: Lightly smoked salmon, or as an apéritif
Vintage years: 2008

6 Ca' dei Frati, I Frati Lugana, Lombardia

This estate has expanded dramatically and raised the bar for the region. By taking a modern approach to vineyard management and lowering yields, the full expression of the Lugana grape shows through in its wines. This wine is particularly vibrant with delicious, ripe, zesty fruit.

Food pairings: Broiled seafood; baked white fish
Vintage years: 2004, 2003, 2001

7 Guerrieri Rizzardi, Chiaretto, Bardolino Classico ®

"Chiaretto" is the Italian form of "clairet," the French word from which we derived our "claret." Like the original clairets, this wine is a deep pink color. Made from local grape varieties, including Corvina, Rondinella, and Molinara, this is a zesty wine full of bright berry and cherry fruit.

Food pairings: Mildly spiced Asian dishes, bouillabaisse
Vintage years: 2008

9 Livio Felluga, Friulano, Colli Orientali del Friuli

Friulano is often identified as Sauvignonasse, a poor relation of Sauvignon Blanc, but in Livio Felluga's hands it creates a rich wine with plenty of tropical fruit and a touch of bitter almond on the finish.

Food pairings: Pork casserole
Vintage years: 2005, 2004, 2001

8 Eugenio Collavini, Broy Bianco, Collio

There's a richness and depth to this wine, derived, in large part, from complex winemaking. Chardonnay and Friulano grapes are dried to concentrate the sugars and then blended with Sauvignon Blanc. The wine is then aged in oak barrels. Terrific balance, concentrated fruit, and a long, seamless finish.

Food pairings: Pasta with beans and cheese
Vintage years: 2004, 2003, 2001

10 Maculan, Torcolato, Breganza ⑤ⓦ 🛢

For three generations, the Maculan family have been making sweet wines in the village of Breganza, in the foothills of the Alps. Their Torcolato, made from raisined Vespaiolo grapes (so-called because their sweetness is said to attract wasps), is rich, intense, and long-lived.

Food pairings: Parmesan and blue cheese; pineapple tarte tatin
Vintage years: 2005, 2004

6   7   8   9   10

Drying grapes, Veneto

Central Italy & Sardinia

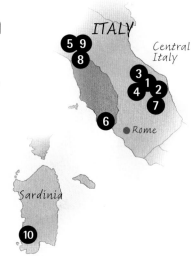

Central Italy's wine regions are divided by the Appenine mountain range, which runs north to south. The contrasts are dramatic—the regions bordering the Adriatic coast on the east are a completely different vinous proposition than those on the Mediterranean coast on the west, especially for white wines. The gently rolling hills of the Marche are the heartland of the Verdicchio grape of Verdicchio dei Castelli dei Jesi fame, a region that has returned to the spotlight in recent years. Meanwhile, over on the Tuscan coast, classic traditional styles rub shoulders with innovative modern wines in a delightfully unpredictable scene.

Vineyard near Matélica, Marche

1 Cantine Belisario, Vigneti del Cero, Verdicchio di Matelica

Verdicchio wines from the Matelica region, south of the more famous Castelli di Jesi, are well worth seeking out. The combination of high altitude and cool nights in Belisario's vineyards allows a long growing season. A dry, tangy, rich wine.

Food pairings: Mushroom risotto, stuffed peppers
Vintage years: 2006, 2005, 2004

2 San Lorenzo, Vigna delle Oche, Verdicchio dei Castelli di Jesi Riserva 🛢

Verdicchio is often dismissed as being another of Italy's neutral white grape varieties, but the best wines from this grape repay aging by developing layers of nutty, honeyed flavors. San Lorenzo's Vigna delle Oche is delicious young, but it's built for the long haul.

Food pairings: Seafood risotto
Vintage years: 2006, 2005, 1997

4 Banfi, San Angelo, Pinot Grigio, Tuscany

This reliable producer is best known for its trio of Brunello di Montalcinos, but it also makes a range of wines based on grapes whose origins lie outside Tuscany. One is the San Angelo Pinot Grigio, a riper, fruitier wine than its more neutral North Italian cousins.

Food pairings: Mild chicken or seafood curries, roast chicken
Vintage years: 2008

3 Casal Farneto, Grancasale, Verdicchio dei Castelli di Jesi Superiore

Casal Farneto's "basic" Verdicchio, the Fontevecchia, is good, but this cuvée is a notch above. Made from grapes harvested quite late in the year, this is a wine with plenty of ripe pineapple and pear fruit, a trace of toasted nuts, and a streak of minerality.

Food pairings: Roast chicken, hard cheeses
Vintage years: 2006, 2005, 2004

5 Poggio al Tesoro, Vermentino Solosole, Bolgheri

Vermentino is a Mediterranean grape, so it's no surprise to find it on the Tuscan coast. Now owned by Verona's Allegrini family, this estate offers a charming wine with classic Vermentino perfume and delicate apricot and tropical fruit. A wine to enjoy in its youth.

Food pairings: Ideal for light weekend lunches
Vintage years: 2008, 2007

6 Fattoria Le Pupille, Solalto, Maremma (Tuscany) ⓢⓦ

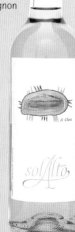

A Tuscan take on Bordeaux Sauternes, Solalto is made from late-harvested Traminer, Sauvignon Blanc, and Semillon grapes allowed to shrivel on the vine before a late fall. The absence of oak allows the delicious flavors of nectarine, apricot, and honey to shine through with supporting zesty freshness.

Food pairings: Fruit pastries, tarte tatin, or savor on its own
Vintage years: 2005

7 Gran Sasso, Pecorino Terre di Chieti, Abruzzi

The Pecorino variety is found only in a small area of Abruzzi and Marche. Marco Flacco's wine is delightfully enticing; he chooses to barrel-ferment around a fifth of the wine in Austrian oak for gentle richness. Charming almond perfume on the nose and crisp fruit on the palate.

Food pairings: An excellent apéritif wine
Vintage years: 2008, 2007

9 Barone Ricasoli, Torricella Chardonnay, Tuscany

Torricella's Chardonnay vineyard is now well established, having been planted in the late 1980s. While the grape isn't local, the character of the wine is truly Tuscan. Over half the wine is aged in new oak for three months, giving complex tropical fruit flavors and a toasty richness.

Food pairings: Full-flavored fish
Vintage years: 2007, 2006

8 Panizzi, Vernaccia di San Gimignano (Tuscany)

This excellent Vernaccia's rich character shows in the wine's brilliant, light yellow color and greenish hue. The pure fruit, unmasked by any oak, combines lime, orchard fruit, and a hint of pineapple in a well-balanced style with excellent persistence and an appealingly savory finish.

Food pairings: Smoked salmon, baked trout
Vintage years: 2008, 2007

10 Santadi, Cala Saliente Vermentino, Sardinia

Light, lemony-scented Vermentino grapes are widely planted in Sardinia; this wine comes from the southwest of the island. Delicate, with good roundness on the palate, it's an unpretentious wine and best enjoyed well-chilled and young.

Food pairings: Seafood galore—Oysters, crayfish, lobster
Vintage years: 2008, 2007

6   7   8   9   10

The Villa Banfi Estate, Montalcino, Tuscany

Southern Italy

There has been a revolution in winemaking in many southern regions that has put both the heel and toe of Italy firmly on the quality wine map. Campania, Puglia, and Sicily are the focus of interest for white wines; the excitement generally surrounds indigenous varieties grown at altitude to escape the extreme heat.

In Sicily, vibrant modern wines are based on grapes such as Inzolia and Grecanico, as well as international grapes well suited to the island's soils and climate. They form an impressive double act with her classic traditional wines. Look for many more inspiring wines to come.

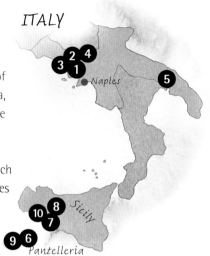

The white town of Locorotondo, Valle Itri, Puglia

1 Vesevo, Fiano di Avellino, Campania

Avellino is often described as one of Italy's most exciting producing areas, due to a combination of poor volcanic soils, high-lying vineyards, and interesting local grapes. This Fiano is fermented at particularly low temperatures (for Italy), and it sees no oak in order to preserve its intense, pure flavor and vibrancy.

Food pairings: The freshest fish possible
Vintage years: 2008, 2007

2 Pietracupa Greco di Trufo, Campania 🆂🛢️

Sabino Loffredo is the name behind the Pietracupa estate, a newcomer that has quickly made an impression. This take on the Greco grape offers intense, sweet aromas and a mineral character typical of the variety. The wine will merit careful cellaring to take on yet more personality.

Food pairings: Lemon sole or sea bream
Vintage years: 2008, 2007

4 Terredora, Loggia della Serra, Greco di Tufo, Campania

Campania's volcanic soil proves fertile ground for Terradora, one of the region's best producers. Although it makes exemplary wines from a number of grapes, this wine, made from Greco di Tufo, stands out for its explosive dried mango and peach flavors, balanced by zesty acidity.

Food pairings: Thai stir-fries
Vintage years: 2008, 2007

3 Vesevo, Sannio Falanghina, Campania

The Falanghina vines at Vesevo's vineyards in Avellino benefit from the cool breeze from the Bay of Naples, allowing the grapes to ripen slowly before harvest in October. This classic variety needs no oak and only minimal winemaking to extract its spiced apple perfume and light honeyed richness.

Food pairings: Fresh broiled sardines
Vintage years: 2008, 2007

5 A Mano Bianco, Puglia

Winemakers Elvezia Sbalchiero and Californian Mark Shannon fell in love with Puglia and now make wine here. They source Fiano and Greco grapes for this lively, zesty wine from the Valle d'Itria, which is cooled by breezes from the Adriatic. A delightful wine for informal drinking.

Food pairings: Roasted herb chicken
Vintage years: 2006, 2003, 2001

6 Donnafugata, Ben Ryé Passito di Pantelleria SW

This exquisite wine is made from low-yielding Zibibbo vines grown on terraces around the island and nurtured carefully. Ben Ryé offers layers of complexity with dried mango and apricot, honey, and a hint of marmalade, complemented by fresh acidity and restrained alcohol.

Food pairings: Best on its own
Vintage years: 2008, 2007

7 Planeta, La Segreta Bianco, Sicily

One of the island's most exciting whites made from a blend of both local and international grapes—Grecanico, Chardonnay, Viognier, and Fiano. The grapes are harvested from August to late September and fermented at low temperatures in stainless steel. Lovely mouthwatering citrus fruit and well structured.

Food pairings: Seafood pasta, salads, or on its own
Vintage years: 2008

9 Pellegrino, Pantelleria Passito Liquoroso SW

This classic sweet wine is made from extremely old Zibibbo vines (Muscat d'Alexandrie). The grapes are dried in the sun, then taken to Pellegrino's modern winery on Pantelleria for vinification and bottling. A delightful golden wine with intense aromas of candied fruit—smooth and persistent.

Food pairings: Fruit pastries
Vintage years: 2008, 2007

8 Tasca d'Almerita, Regaleali Le Rose, Sicily R

The impressive range from this estate includes this charming light red rosé. Two leading stars in the Sicilian red grape constellation—Nero d'Avola and Nerello Mascalese—give this wine great local personality; the wine has juicy, fresh, strawberry and red cherry fruit and a structured, food-friendly style.

Food pairings: Broiled fish, salads; or on its own
Vintage years: 2008

10 Planeta, Rosé, Sicily R

With four wineries distributed across the island, Planeta is one of Sicily's biggest names. Although it produces quantity, it is as a quality producer that Planeta shines. Even its rosé, an afterthought for many winemakers, is made with attention to detail, providing pretty flavors of pomegranates and strawberries.

Food pairings: Calamari alla plancha, seafood salads, barbecued salmon
Vintage years: 2008

Vineyard near Alcamo, Sicily

Galicia

●León

●Pamplona

Rioja &
Navarra

Vila Real ●

Castilla y León

Catalunya

Vinho
Verde

●Barcelona

Douro

Beiras

Dão

●Madrid

PORTUGAL

SPAIN

●Lisbon

Alentejo

Sherry, Montilla
& Malaga

Spain & Portugal

A new generation of Spanish winemakers has turned the spotlight on the country's best indigenous white grapes. Thanks to modern winemaking techniques, thrilling white wines made from grapes such as Albariño, Verdejo, and Godello have emerged from Spanish regions in the cooler northwest of the country, while regions to the north and northeast offer wines in a variety of different guises, sometimes with the benefit of short oak aging.

Portugal boasts an even wider range of local grapes for an equally noteworthy array of white wines. This corner of the Iberian peninsula is influenced by three climatic conditions—Atlantic, Mediterranean, and continental—which define each region's wine style.

Both Spain and Portugal have a colorful palette of red grapes to draw on for their food-friendly rosé wines. They also boast unique fortified wines and sweet wines, which are often very affordable.

Galicia & Castilla y León, Spain

Galicia's Rías Baixas is home to Spain's most prized white wines. The Albariño grape excels here, and vines are traditionally grown on pergolas to protect them from the wet conditions. In Rueda, to the west of Castilla y León, Verdejo and Sauvignon Blanc grapes are routinely harvested at night in the quest for higher quality. Meanwhile, the Godello grape of Valdeorras is enjoying a renaissance. Oak is used sparingly here; in the hands of a talented winemaker the grapes are more than capable of offering great wines without it.

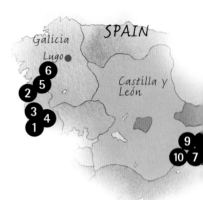

Sauvignon Blanc grapes are routinely harvested at night

1 Bodegas Terras Gauda, Terras Gauda, Rías Baixas

Terras Gauda owes its distinctive character to the blending of three of the region's grapes—Albariño, Loureira, and Caiño Blanco—harvested consecutively each fall. The wine style is structured and aromatic with elegant, peachy fruit and a hint of lemon.

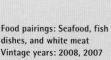

Food pairings: Seafood, fish dishes, and white meat
Vintage years: 2008, 2007

2 Condes de Albarei, Rías Baixas

This Albariño, made from grapes from the Salnés Valley with a combination of traditional viticulture and modern techniques, is a fresh wine with delicate citrus fruit presented in an unpretentious style—an ideal introduction to the Albariño grape in the Rías Baixas.

Food pairings: Seafood, baked white fish and white meat
Vintage years: 2008, 2007

4 Lagar de Cervera Albariño, Rías Baixas

This Albariño is made from grapes from Lagar de Cervera's own vineyards at O Rosal and Cambados. Winemaking ensures the careful balancing of acidity and alcohol, resulting in a charming wine with typical Albariño character; fresh, well-structured, with an elegant finish.

Food pairings: Seafood, fish, rice dishes, or savor alone
Vintage years: 2008, 2007

3 Pazo de Señoráns, Pazo Señoráns, Rías Baixas

A consistently excellent wine from a highly rated Rías Baixas producer, Pazo Señoráns is also an incredibly pure example of the character of the Albariño grape with floral aromas, vibrant white peach and melon fruit, and refreshing acidity.

Food pairings: Seafood, especially shellfish and fleshy white fish
Vintage years: 2008, 2007

5 Valdamor Albariño, Rías Baixas

Using grapes from vineyards up to 120 years old in the Salnés area, this is a particularly rich style of Albariño and a delightful food-friendly wine. It is ready to drink soon after bottling and will also benefit from a year or two in the bottle.

Food pairings: Seafood stews, baked fish, rice dishes, white meat
Vintage years: 2008, 2007

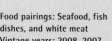

6 Nava Real Verdejo, Rueda

The vineyards for this fine Rueda wine are located 2,000-plus feet above sea level. The high altitude, together with vineyard practices that encourage low yields and early ripening, result in a wine that is the perfect combination of freshness, concentration, and finesse.

Food pairings: Fish, chicken, salads, rice dishes, or as apéritif
Vintage years: 2008, 2007

7 Bodegas Aura, Aura Verdejo, Rueda

Verdejo is the main grape in this wine, but the addition of some Sauvignon Blanc possibly accounts for this wine's impressive style. Delicate herbaceous fruit character and lively apple and pear flavors can be enjoyed right to the bottom of the glass. Consistently one of the best wines of the region.

Food pairings: Seafood, smoked fish, lightly spiced dishes, or as apéritif
Vintage years: 2008, 2007

9 Gaba do Xil Godello, Valdeorras

Made from a combination of trellised and older traditional bush vines from terraced, inland slopes, Winemaker Telmo Rodríguez opts for no oak, allowing the flavor of the Godello grape to shine through. It is dry, refreshing, with apple fruit flavors, and a hint of minerality.

Food pairings: Fish, meat, rice dishes, salads, or as apéritif
Vintage years: 2008, 2007

8 Naia Verdejo, Rueda

Bodegas Naia is located in La Seca, which features some of the best soils for vines in the region. Naia is a Verdejo with great character, thanks to four months aging on the lees before bottling. Lots of bright white fruit on the palate, supported by tangy, refreshing acidity.

Food pairings: Fish, chicken, lightly spiced foods, or as aperitif
Vintage years: 2008, 2007

10 Valdesil Godello, Valdeorras

The grapes for Valdesil Godello come from vineyards in the area of Vilamartín de Valdeorras. The wine is released after several months in the bottle and the style is rich and complex. A sophisticated wine to enjoy now or after a few years in the bottle.

Food pairings: Baked fish and poultry
Vintage years: 2008, 2007, 2006

The "Solero" process—after harvesting, the grapes are placed in the sun for several days in order to increase sugar content and reduce the malic acid and tannin content

Rioja, Navarra & Somontano, Spain

Rioja's white wines have been a point of interest since winemakers began to experiment with oak to enhance the flavors of the region's rather timid grapes, namely Viura and Malvasía. Meanwhile, Navarra and Somontano have taken an altogether modern approach. Here you are more likely to find an impressive Spanish take on Chardonnay, which is well suited to higher vineyards in both regions. Navarra also offers a treasure trove of sweet wines that are well worth seeking out.

SPAIN

Pamplona

Rioja, Navarra & Somontano

Señorio de Sarria Vineyards, Navarra

1 Olvena Chardonnay, Somontano

This family-run winery is part of this young region's forward-looking team of producers. Most of the must is fermented in stainless steel. A small portion is fermented in French oak and blended into the final wine, giving it delicate tropical fruit and lemon flavors and fine aromas.

Food pairings: Fish, poultry, rice dishes, or as apéritif
Vintage years: 2008, 2007

2 Señorío de Sarría Rosado, Navarra R

Winemaker Milagros Rodríguez uses Garnacha grapes, the traditional grape for rosé in Navarra, but takes a thoroughly modern approach when it comes to style. This rosé, as vibrant and fresh as its raspberry color, makes a great introduction to the region's contemporary wine styles for everyday drinking.

Food pairings: Light salads, pasta dishes, and barbecue meals
Vintage years: 2008, 2007

4 Señorío de Sarría Moscatel Dulce, Navarra Sw

Señorío de Sarría sources the grapes for this Moscatel in the hot and dry southern area near Corella, the preferred location for the variety in Navarra. It has citrus and tropical fruit aromas, honey and lemon flavors, with balancing acidity.

Food pairings: Foie gras; soft cheeses
Vintage years: 2008, 2007

3 Ochoa Moscatel, Navarra Sw

Father–daughter team Javier and Adriana Ochoa pick the Moscatel grapes from their south-facing vineyard at Finca de Traibuenas when they have reached the perfect stage of ripeness. The wine is an excellent expression of its grape variety, with delicious, fresh, juicy, grapey flavors; perfectly balanced sweetness; and an elegant dry finish.
Food pairings: Desserts and blue cheeses, or savor on its own
Vintage years: 2008, 2007

5 Finca Allende Rioja Blanco

A sophisticated white Rioja also made from Viura and Malvasía grapes from vines at least 35 years old. The grapes are hand-picked, sorted, and lightly pressed before passing into new French barrels for fermentation and aging, giving this wine impressive complexity.
Food pairings: Smoked chicken, cured meats, pâté, fish, and chicken stews
Vintage years: 2008, 2007

6 Cosme Palacio Blanco, Rioja

A good example of a Rioja white made from Viura grapes. The character of the grape is enhanced by six months in new French oak barrels, giving the wine hints of pineapple, citrus, and vanilla and good balancing acidity.

Food pairings: Seafood, smoked fish, rice dishes, pâté, and cheese
Vintage years: 2008, 2007

7 Muga Blanco, Rioja

This fine Rioja white, a blend of mostly Viura with a smaller amount of Malvasía, is made from grapes sourced in the Rioja Alta area in the Oja and Tirón River Valleys. Muga Blanco offers an attractive creamy texture, subtle pineapple and apple flavors, and mouthwatering acidity. Very food-friendly.

Food pairings: Cured meats, pâté, fish and chicken stews, mature cheeses
Vintage years: 2008, 2007

8 Castillo de Maetierra, Libalis, Rioja

The three grape varieties—Moscatel, Viura, and Malvasía—making up this original off-dry wine come from vineyards on terraces overlooking the Ebro River in the south of the Rioja region. Fermentation takes place at a low temperature to extract the wine's aromas and its natural sweetness.

Food pairings: Foie gras, pâté, fish and chicken dishes
Vintage years: 2008, 2007

9 Cune Rosado, Rioja Ⓡ

This classic Rioja rosé is made from Tempranillo grapes picked when they reach optimum ripeness. Juice is extracted by the saignée (free-run) method before fermentation, which lasts for about eight days. A delightful rosé with juicy red summer fruit and good length.

Food pairings: Rice and pasta dishes, salads, charcuterie, and roast vegetables
Vintage years: 2008, 2007

10 Marqués de Cáceres Rosé, Rioja Ⓡ

Marqués de Cáceres sources the Tempranillo and Garnacha grapes from the cooler northern Rioja Alta for this thirst-quenching rosé. The wine is bottled young to preserve its lively red berry flavors. A rosé to enjoy with or without food year-round.

Food pairings: Salad niçoise, creamy pasta dishes, charcuterie
Vintage years: 2008, 2007

Somontano, Spanish wine region in Aragón

Catalunya & the Mediterranean, Spain

The white wines of Spain's Mediterranean regions are particularly diverse and versatile. Winemaking regulations are more liberal in this region and, as a result, local varieties grow side by side with their foreign cousins, so you can find Moscatel and Gewürztraminer in the same blend. This is also Spain's sparkling wine heartland. Grapes for cava wines are grown throughout Catalonia. Cavas are produced according to the traditional method (second fermentation takes place in the bottle).

Vines growing near Valdepeñas, Spain

① Torres, Viña Esmeralda, Catalunya

This eclectic white is made from Moscatel with a small amount of Gewürztraminer. The wine is unoaked, allowing it to express a myriad of flavors—a hint of honeysuckle on the nose while flavors of apricot and lychee mingle on the palate with a touch of spice.

Food pairings: Seafood, pâté, lightly spiced foods, or as apéritif
Vintage years: 2008, 2007

② Castillo Perelada Roc Blanco, Empordà

A good example of the light, fragrant white wines found along Spain's Mediterranean coast. The vineyards are in the region of Empordà, which touches the French border in northern Catalonia. Two grapes, Xarel-lo and Muscat, harmonize to produce a pale lemon-colored wine with tangy fruit—unoaked.

Food pairings: A perfect apéritif, lovely with fish and chicken
Vintage years: 2008, 2007

④ Albet i Noya Brut Reserva Cava ⓈⓅ

Albet i Noya makes this Brut Reserva from Chardonnay and the three traditional cava grapes and ages the blend for at least 18 months on the lees. A refreshing and elegant cava with well-balanced fruit and acidity.

Food pairings: Canapés, smoked salmon blinis, light foods, salads
Vintage years: NV

③ Celler de Joan Sangenis, Mas d'en Compte, Priorat

Priorat is largely red wine country, but this is one of its white gems. Joan Sangenis insists on indigenous varieties—Garnacha, Picapoll, Pansá, and Macabeo—but there's a modern twist in the use of mostly French oak for fermentation and lees aging. A wine with great local character.

Food pairings: Baked fish, chicken casseroles, mature cheese
Vintage years: 2008, 2007

⑤ Codorníu Pinot Noir Cava Ⓡ ⓈⓅ

Codorniu's sizeable plantings of Pinot Noir in the Lleida region go into this fragrant rosé cava. The grapes are picked at night to ensure the fruit is in peak condition. Enjoy within a year of purchase to fully appreciate its vibrant red summer fruit flavors.

Food pairings: Canapés, salmon, sashimi, light summer meals, barbecues
Vintage years: NV

6 Torres, Fransola, Penedès

An elegant white from the eponymous estate in high-lying Penedès, where cold nights allow the concentration of flavors in the Sauvignon Blanc and Parellada grapes. Fransola is partially fermented in new oak barrels, giving the wine a lovely structure and the ability to develop over a few years.

Food pairings: Broiled and baked fish, poultry, mild cheeses
Vintage years: 2008, 2007, 2006

7 Albet i Noya, Lignum Blanc, Penedès

The Chardonnay grapes in this blend are fermented and aged for a short period in oak, while the Sauvignon Blanc grapes are fermented in stainless steel vats. The wine has an attractive lemony richness on the palate; its more complex style makes it ideal for food pairing.

Food pairings: Fried and baked fish, light meats, and cheese
Vintage years: 2008, 2007

9 Castillo Perelada Brut Reserva Cava, Penedès **Sp**

A delightful cava made from the trio of cava grapes—Macabeo, Xarel-lo, and Parellada—sourced in the Penedès region. The base wines are aged on the lees for 12 to 15 months, giving the wine an attractive slightly creamy texture.

Food pairings: Canapés, smoked salmon blinis, light foods, salads
Vintage years: NV

8 Albet i Noya, Xarel-lo Classic, Penedès

The truly local Xarel-lo grape stars in this wine from Albet i Noya, a producer practicing organic viticulture in the heart of Penedès. The grapes come from south-facing slopes at Costers de l'Ordal. Fresh and lively with ripe peach flavors, it is bottled fresh from the tank after vinification and light filtration. Unoaked.

Food pairings: Light salads, fish, and meat
Vintage years: 2008, 2007

10 Gran Caus Rosado, Penedès **R**

An intriguing deep-colored Merlot rosé from an avant-garde producer. Dry, savory, with lots of juicy red fruit, it has a structured style. As the label says: "A rosé for people who don't like rosé." Chill for half an hour and serve in a big glass with food.

Food pairings: Chorizo and other charcuterie, salads, and barbecued food
Vintage years: 2008, 2007

Sant Sadurní d'Anoia, in "Cava country," Penedès

Sherry, Montilla &
Malaga, Spain

Sherry takes its name from its place of origin, Jerez, one of Spain's most charming and hospitable winemaking towns, in the southwest. This is the best place to learn how these intriguing wines are made; from light Manzanillas and Finos to more powerful Amontillados. In the southeast, other sweet and fortified wines are equally recommendable. Montilla producers follow tradition, preserving the distinctive character of their fortified wines. There is also renewed interest in the light Moscatel wines of Málaga as modern viticultural practices are putting this region back on the map.

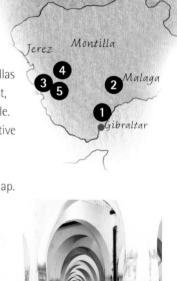

Jerez de la Frontera, Montilla

1 Bodegas Alvear, Solera 1927 Pedro Ximénez, Montilla Moriles 🆂🆆

This mahogany-colored sweet dessert wine is made from Pedro Ximénez, the star grape of the region. Some grapes are sun-dried, giving the must concent-rated raisin flavors before maturation over at least of five years in a solera system.

Food pairings: Ice cream, chocolate
Vintage years: NV

2 Ordoñez No. 1 Selección Especial, Málaga 🆂🆆

A stunning sweet wine made from old-vine Moscatel grapes left to over-ripen on the hillsides of Almáchar in the region of Málaga. Pale lemon in color, incredibly pure, and fresh with delicate mandarin fruit flavors. Long, elegant, and impeccably made.

Food pairings: Orange or lemon desserts, or savor on its own
Vintage years: 2008, 2007

4 Harveys Fino, Jerez

The Palomino grapes for this classic fino come from the Jerez Superior area. The wine is aged in "very seasoned" American oak butts, according to the traditional solera system. Bone-dry with a lovely yeasty tang, great length, and intensity.

Food pairings: Toasted almonds, olives, seafood, charcuterie
Vintage years: NV

3 Lustau Los Arcos Dry Amontillado, Jerez

The Palomino grape appears in many guises in Jerez; here, it's a fine Amontillado, Fino's slightly older sibling. It has a tempting nutty aroma and soft raisin flavors on the palate. Delightful to the last drop, serve it chilled to enjoy it at its best.

Food pairings: Tapas, charcuterie
Vintage years: NV

5 Bodegas Hidalgo-La Gitana, La Gitana Manzanilla, Jerez

Manzanilla sherries, the lightest style within the sherry family, come from producers in the charming whitewashed town of Sanlúcar de Barrameda. La Gitana, "the gypsy," is a good example of the dry, fresh, tangy style.

Food pairings: Fresh sardines, fried squid, garlic shrimp
Vintage years: NV

Vinho Verde and Beiras, Portugal

The lush northern Minho region takes in the Vinho Verde wine area where the lightest Portuguese whites are produced. The Atlantic coast and high rainfall influences the style, but the granitic soils also account for a crisp edge to wines. Quality has improved in recent years, thanks to the wider adoption of higher caliber grapes; Alvarinho performs well in carefully chosen sites and the aromatic Loureiro now has a prominent role in Vinho Verde blends. A little farther south, Beiras is also good territory for whites with great personality. Seek them out for weekend lunches.

Densely planted vineyards in the Minho region

1 Quinta de Soalheiro, Soalheiro Alvarinho, Vinho Verde

This producer has pioneered the Alvarinho grape variety in recent years at vineyard sites near Melgaço, close to the Spanish border. Soalheiro Alvarinho comes from a sheltered valley where grapes ripen early, allowing winemakers Antonio and Luis Cerdeira to make a surprisingly intense, full-bodied style for this region.

Food matches: Fish casseroles, white meat, salads
Vintage years: 2008, 2007

2 Anselmo Mendes, Muros Antigos Alvarinho, Vinho Verde

Anselmo Mendes has a hand in making many Alvarinho wines —the locals refer to him as Mr. Alvarinho. This is a good introduction to his range; it has a pale lemon color, plenty of delicate tropical fruit on the palate, and an elegant finish.

Food matches: Seafood; broiled fish
Vintage years: 2008, 2007

4 Quinta da Aveleda, Aveleda Alvarinho, Vinho Verde

A stylish wine made from a careful selection of grapes from vineyards in the Monção region. Dry and refreshing with floral aromas and flavors of ripe peach, tropical fruit, and a hint of spice mingling on the palate.

Food matches: Baked or broiled fish and chicken
Vintage years: 2008, 2007

3 Quinta das Arcas, Arca Nova, Vinho Verde

A charming light-bodied Vinho Verde made by Fernando Machado from Loureiro and Arinto grapes. The wine is aromatic and lively on the nose, with light citrus fruit on the palate. It is best young, but it will develop for up to two years after bottling.

Food matches: Shellfish, fish, lightly spiced Asian food
Vintage years: 2008, 2007

5 Luis Pato Maria Gomes, Beiras

Luis Pato is highly respected for his work with indigenous grapes. He makes wine under the less restrictive Vinho Regional classification to achieve his distinctive wine styles. The unoaked Maria Gomes, featuring the grape of the same wine, has delightful minerally freshness.

Food matches: Oysters, scallops, baked cod
Vintage years: 2008, 2007

Other regions of Portugal

High altitude coupled with granite, schist, and slate soils give the wines of Dão and the particularly scenic Douro a surprising elegance. Wherever you are, there's a different grape to discover; winemakers here have a knack of exploiting their natural resources, and the array of climates and soils give great diversity to the wines. Toward the south, in regions such as the Ribatejo and the Alentejo, the soils are likely to be sand and clay-based and the wine styles are generally softer and more alcoholic. Local grapes, including the lively Antão Vaz steal the show.

A small vineyard in Vale de Mendiz, Douro

1 Quinta dos Roques Encruzado, Dão

Encruzado, the star native grape of the Dão region, is capable of structured white wines, and this is a fine example. Over half the wine is fermented in French oak barrels, which brings out the grape's fine white pear fruit character and gives the wine good complexity.

Food pairings: Fish stews, broiled seafood, lightly spiced cuisine
Vintage years: 2008, 2007

2 Sogrape, Planalto, Douro

Planalto, a well-known Douro wine, is made from Malvasia, Viosinho, Gouveio, and Códgea grapes sourced from high-altitude vineyards. This food-friendly, full-bodied wine with lovely complexity on the palate and passion fruit and pineapple flavors will develop for up to two years in the bottle.

Food pairings: Smoked salmon, white meat, fishcakes
Vintage years: 2008, 2007

4 Quinta da Lagoalva, Espirito Lagoalva Branco, Ribatejo

Made from five grapes—Alvarinho, Arinto, Fernão Pires, Sauvignon Blanc, and Verdelho. Harvested at night to achieve the freshest fruit possible, each variety is vinified separately before blending. Lemon and tropical fruit flavors with refreshing acidity.

Food pairings: Broiled fish, creamy pasta dishes, soft cheeses
Vintage years: 2008, 2007

3 Sogrape, Pena de Pato Rosé, Douro Ⓡ

A vibrant raspberry-pink rosé with good structure. Its lively raspberry and strawberry fruit flavors are characteristic of Douro rosés made from Touriga Nacional and Touriga Franca grapes. Enjoy this wine in its youth, although it has the structure to last for a couple of years if cellared carefully.

Food pairings: Salmon, trout, pasta dishes, salads
Vintage years: 2008, 2007

5 Herdade do Esporão, Esporão Reserva Branco, Alentejo

This wine from the heart of Portugal's cork-growing country, is made from Antão Vaz, Roupeiro, and Arinto. It spends a short period in new American and French oak barrels, but the three grapes shine through in an impressive southern white.

Food pairings: Broiled shellfish, baked sea bass
Vintage years: 2007, 2006

Madeira

The Madeira wine style was discovered by accident over 400 years ago when it was found that casks of wine mellowed and became delightful in subtropical heat—either on ships crossing the equator or in the lofts of Madeiran houses. Today the artificial heat of the *estufa* (hot store) replicates the process for most Madeira wines. Four grapes are used: Sercial to make the driest wines, Verdelho for slightly sweeter wines, and Bual and Malmsey (Malvasia) for the sweetest styles. Madeira wines can age for decades and are often described as indestructible.

Vines growing near Camara de Lobos, Madeira

1 Barbeito Single Cask Malvasia 44a 2000

The Malvasia grapes were harvested in 2000. The wine in cask 44a evolved in a particularly interesting way and exceeded expectations during the high temperatures of 2007 and a long hot summer. It was bottled in early 2008. A golden, rich, and opulent wine with concentrated honey flavors.

Food pairings: No food required, just a few wine-loving friends
Vintage years: 2000

2 Henriques & Henriques 10-Year-Old Sercial

The Sercial grapes are picked from mid-August to October. The following spring the wine spends three months in an estufa where it is heated to around 133°F. At least three months in oak barrels gives a dry, fresh wine with hints of brown spice and citrus peel.

Food pairings: Serve as an apéritif and surprise your friends
Vintage years: NV

4 Madeira Wine Company, Blandy's 5-Year-Old Bual

One of the minority of Madeira wines that is aged in the traditional canteiro system rather than the estufa; gently heated naturally in the lofts of the lodges in Funchal over a number of years. A medium-bodied wine with subtle vanilla and toffee flavors.

Food pairings: Dried fruit, hard cheeses; an after-dinner wine
Vintage years: NV

3 Henriques & Henriques 15-Year-Old Verdelho

Madeira wines made from Verdelho start life as their Sercial siblings do, but they gain more complexity as they age. This wine has an attractive light brown color with an orange hue. Its nutty and fresh orange citric flavors are beautifully balanced with a delicate sweetness.

Food pairings: Aromatic dark chocolate and pastries
Vintage years: NV

5 Madeira Wine Company, Blandy's 15-Year-Old Malmsey

This Malmsey wine is also aged in the canteiro style, with barrels gently moved from the warmer, higher floors of a loft to the cooler, lower floors as it matures. The reward is a full-bodied, smooth wine, with dried fruit, hints of chocolate, and citrus peel.

Food pairings: Sip slowly and enjoy to the last drop
Vintage years: NV

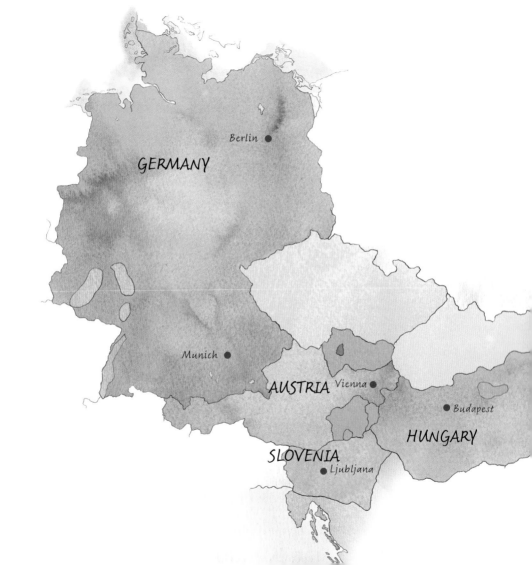

Central & Eastern Europe

Taken as a whole, the countries of Central and Eastern Europe offer a huge variety of wine styles. Many of them can be discovered only by visiting their wine regions and exploring wines along with the local gastronomy.

The wines of Germany and Austria are comparatively well represented outside their borders. Meanwhile, their lesser-known neighbors have white wines of interest for the visitor.

Swiss producers are particularly successful with the white Chasselas grape, while producers in the Czech Republic and Slovakia are making much improved whites from varieties such as Welschriesling, Rhine Riesling, Sylvaner, and Grüner Veltliner. In the former Yugoslavia, Slovenia is one to watch as well as Croatia; some of the most interesting whites are made from the islands along the Adriatic coast from local grapes such as Posip, Vugava, and Marastina. The region of Istria, close to Slovenia, is also noteworthy for wines made from Malvasia.

In Romania, white wine is far more important than red, and there seems to be good potential for development. Moldova, situated in the northeast of the country, is the most important region and home to a botrytized wine named after the region of Cotnari. Can this wine do for Romania what Tokaji has done for Hungary (see page 270)?

1 Mosel, Saar &
Ruwer Valleys

2 Rheingau

3 Nahe

4 Rheinhessen & Pflaz

GERMANY

The wines are all produced
around rivers, mainly the
Rhine and its tributaries,
often sheltered by mountains.
The rivers have significant
microclimate effects to
moderate the temperature.
Soil here is slate to absorb
the sun's heat and retain
it overnight. German wine
regions are some of the most
northerly in the world.

Germany

Germany has 13 wine regions and over 370,000 acres of vineyards, most of them located at the northern limits for winemaking. However, thanks to a unique combination of climate, soils, and grape, a dazzling array of wines can be found here.

Riesling is Germany's grape par excellence; hardly any other variety is found in high profile regions such as the Mosel, Rheingau, Nahe, and Pfalz. The grape is capable of producing a colorful palette of styles; they are generally light and ranging from dry or off-dry Kabinetts to late-harvest styles, and even eiswines when conditions permit. The best vintages are proclaimed when the balance between acidity and sugar is optimal, allowing the rich, honeyed, and often minerally character of the fruit to express itself in a refreshing wine style.

German wines can appear baffling to the novice, but they are well worth discovering. They can also present a challenge when it comes to food pairing. Why not indulge in a glass of golden nectar on its own?

Mosel, Saar & Ruwer Valleys

The Mosel Valley, flanked by the Saar and Ruwer Valleys, is the epicenter of German wine. Each valley has its own style, but fragrant aromas, light elegance, and fresh acidity are common characteristics. Mosel offers striking scenery as it winds its way from its Vosges Mountain source to meet the Rhine at Koblenz. The best slopes are those with southern exposure and sharp gradients. Ancient vines can be found in this area of Europe as it has always been resistant to phylloxera.

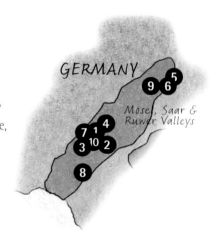

Sunset over Trittenheim, Mosel-Saar-Ruwer

1 Dr. Loosen, Wehlener Sonnenuhr Riesling Spätlese

This striking, rocky vineyard has two outstanding features: its remarkably steep gradient and pure blue slate soils. Its wines are characterized by a lively minerality and fine acidity balancing citrus and ripe peach fruit flavors. Try the Spätlese, then explore the other levels of sweetness.

Food pairings: Tarte tatin
Vintage years: 2008, 2007

2 Dr. Loosen, Bernkasteler Lay Riesling Kabinett

Soils of the Bernkasteler Lay vineyard, located near the village of Bernkastel, are predominantly slate, and the established vines here produce wines with a rich texture and expressive character. Kabinett wines, from grapes picked early in the harvest, are the specialty and, in much smaller quantities, Eiswein.

Food pairings: Poultry or pork
Vintage years: 2009, 2008, 2007

4 Weingut JJ Prüm, Wehlener Sonnenuhr Riesling Auslese

Prüm wines are highly regarded in the Mosel, especially those from the Sonnenuhr "sundial vineyard" across the river from the town of Wehlen. The grapes make honed, complex, elegant Rieslings that age gracefully—especially the Auslese style.

Food pairings: Fois gras, apple or apricot pastries
Vintage years: 2007, 2006

3 St Urbans-hof, Estate Riesling

Run by Nik Weis, grandson of the founder, St Urbans-Hof's sizeable vineyards are mainly located on the slopes of the Mosel and Saar Valleys. The crisp, dry Estate Riesling comes from the Saar "Wiltinger Schlangengraben" vineyard, an ideal source of grapes for refreshing, light Riesling wines. Fermented with natural yeast.

Food pairings: Enjoy as an apéritif
Vintage years: 2007, 2006

5 Kendermanns Riesling Spätlese

This modern Spätlese is made from grapes with a high sugar content, which are harvested at the end of September. It is fermented in stainless steel rather than traditional oak casks to preserve as much fruit flavor as possible. Fresh with bright, sweet, white peach fruit and balancing acidity.

Food pairings: Fusion food; slightly sweet and spicy dishes
Vintage years: 2008, 2007

6 Kendermanns Leiwener Laurentiuslay Riesling Beerenauslese Sw

The Leiwener Laurentiuslay vineyard, close to the Mosel, allows the development of botrytis in certain vintages. Grapes are gently pressed and fermented for around six weeks. The wine is complex and elegant, sweet, and smooth, with apricot, mango, and gentle alcohol.

Food pairings: Apple pie; blue cheese
Vintage years: 2005

7 Weingut Max Ferd Richter, Wehlener Sonnenuhr Riesling Kabinett

Established for over 300 years, this producer acquired sites in the famous Wehlener Sonnenuhr vineyard in the 1970s. Its Riesling Kabinett is elegant, with delicate fruit, typical of wines from the area. Watch for other styles including Spätlese wines.

Food pairings: Asparagus with hollandaise sauce, on its own
Vintage years: 2007

9 Beate Knebel, Winninger Röttgen Riesling Auslese Sw

The Knebel family, based at Koblenz, can trace their vine-growing history back to 1650. Their emphasis is quality: key aspects are very low yields and the use of wild yeasts. Their wines, especially sweeter Auslese wines from the Röttgen vineyard, have a wonderful complexity.

Food pairings: Instead of dessert
Vintage years: 2007

8 Van Volxem Saar Riesling

Current owner Roman Niewodniczanski has restored this historic Wiltingen estate to its former glory, imposing his own style; late-harvest, low-yield wines that express their origin. Saar Riesling, a dry, medium-bodied wine, has lovely intensity and good length—a good introduction to the range.

Food pairings: A refreshing apéritif wine
Vintage years: 2007

10 Selbach-Oster, Zeltinger Sonnenuhr Riesling Beerenauslese 🛢

The Selbach-Oster estate is run by husband and wife Johannes and Barbara Selbach. Situated in the Mittel Mosel area, their vineyards include holdings in the prime Zeltinger Sonnenuhr. Their Beerenauslese is rich with apricot, peach, and lime flavors. Enjoy now or cellar carefully.

Food pairings: Savor on its own
Vintage years: 2006

Sundial amidst the vines, Upper Mosel

Rheingau

Bordering the Rhine from Gisenheim to Eltville am Rhein, the Rheingau is home to some of Germany's most prestigious estates. It is sheltered by the Taunus hills to the north, and the influence of the river to the south has a warming effect that encourages botrytis. For many centuries this region has been associated with Riesling wines. While many dry styles can be found today, it also has a long established reputation as the source of some of the country's greatest sweet wines; indeed, the importance of harvesting at different stages of ripeness was first recognized here.

Looking out over vineyards from Schloss Johannisberg, Geisenheim, Rheingau

1 Leitz, Eins Zwei Dry

This is the latest addition to the portfolio from the Josef Leitz estate located at Rudesheim and specializing in Riesling wines. Made by Johannes Leitz, who made his first vintage in 1985, this dry Riesling has delicious, tangy lime and apple fruit. Well made and fairly priced.

Food pairings: White fish or poultry; an ideal apéritif wine
Vintage years: 2009, 2008

2 Prinz, Hallgartener Jungfer Goldkapsel Riesling Spätlese ⓢⓦ

Fred Prinz, assisted by his wife Sabine, has turned his hobby into a full-time winemaking venture at Hallgarten. Their vineyards are around the villages of Schonhell for drier styles, and Jungfer for fruitier and sweeter styles. Yields are kept low and the style is very honed, as this Spätlese shows.

Food pairings: Foie gras, blue cheese, or enjoy on its own
Vintage years: 2007

4 Balthasar Ress, Hattenheimer Schützenhaus Reisling Kabinett

This winery, run by Christian and Stefan Ress, is a leading player in the Rheingau, with an extensive portfolio of single vineyard and cru wines. This wine has peachy, citrussy flavors, with a touch of residual sugar.

Food pairings: Chicken tagine or as an apéritif
Vintage years: 2007, 2006

3 Schloss Johannisberg Riesling Spätlese ⓢⓦ

This majestic estate is steeped in history—even Napoleon is named as a former owner. The first botrytis-affected wine was made here in 1775 when grapes with gray rot were separated from those with desirable noble rot. Late harvest wines a specialty today, including Spätlese styles.

Food pairings: Blue cheese or savor on its own
Vintage years: 2007

5 Robert Weil, Kiedricher Grafenberg Riesling Auslese ⓢⓦ

This estate, run by Wilhelm Weil, grandson of the founder, includes 27 acres in the prized Kiedricher Gräfenberg area. Its sunny, sheltered conditions have allowed Rieslings with all levels of sweetness to be made since 1989. The intensely rich Auslese has great finesse.

Food pairings: Enjoy on its own
Vintage years: 2007

Other German regions

Riesling again steals much of the limelight in regions such as the Pfalz, Nahe, and Rheinhessen, though each region and producer offers a slightly different take on the variety. A rich choice of soils often holds the key. In the Nahe region, for instance, vineyards are planted on volcanic, sandstone, clay, or slate soils, depending on location, making this one of Germany's most interesting regions. In the more continental Franconia, Riesling struggles to ripen. Other varieties, including Silvaner and Scheurebe, are better suited to the climate, making this region worth exploring for a more diverse choice of grape varieties.

Rows of vines with flowering almond trees, Siebeldingen, Palatinate

1 Villa Wolf Silvaner, Pfalz

This Wachenheim estate has been enjoying a new lease of life under the ownership of Ernst Loosen; traditional Pfalz wines with plenty of character are its hallmark. The floral Silvaner offers savory dryness and crisp white fruit in a pure, clean style. A versatile food wine.

Food pairings: Smoked fish, turkey, and salads
Vintage years: 2007

2 Dr. Bürklin-Wolf, Bürkin Estate Riesling, Pfalz

Run by Bettina Bürklin-von Guradze since 1990 along with the Gasthaus Zur Kanne restaurant, this estate is run on a Burgundian-style vineyard classification and biodynamic viticulture is practiced. This wine—dry, crisp, and fruity with apple and spice flavors—is a good starting point.
Food pairings: Fusion cuisine and mildly spicy foods
Vintage years: 2004

4 Schäfer-Fröhlich, Bockenauer Felseneck Riesling Spätlese Trocken, Nahe

Tim Schäfer-Fröhlich is extracts the full potential of Riesling at the family's vineyards through low yields, wild yeast, and biodynamic viticulture. The steep slope of Felseneck has volcanic soils, which give this dry wine its acidity and enhance its lime fruit.

Food pairings: Savor on its own
Vintage years: 2005

3 Reichsrat von Buhl, Forster Ungeheurer Riesling Auslese, Pfalz

Owned by Baron von und zu Guttenberg, Reichsrat von Buhl has vineyard holdings in the villages of Forst, Deidesheim, and Ruppertsberg. Winemaker Frank John favors fruit-driven wines, which are very appealing in their youth. The Auslese is medium- to full-bodied with modest alcohol—good cellaring potential.

Food pairings: Cheesecake
Vintage years: 2007

5 Schneider, Melaphyr Riesling Trocken, Nahe

Jakob Schneider, who studied winemaking in Geisenheim and is one of the rising stars in the Nahe, has taken over the small family winery at Niederhausen. He is assisted by other family members, including grandmother Liesel. Try the spicy, minerally Melaphyr dry Riesling; the sweeter wines are also excellent.

Food pairings: White meats, salads
Vintage years: 2007, 2006

6 Kendermanns Riesling Rheinhessen

The grapes for this Riesling wine are sourced from growers along the Rhine, who are encouraged to practice environmentally friendly viticulture; harvest usually takes place in mid-October. The must is fermented in stainless steel and remains on the lees until January. An aromatic wine with a good weight of tangy fruit on the palate.

Food pairings: Lemon chicken, Dover sole, trout, or as an apéritif
Vintage years: 2009, 2008

7 Wittmann, Morstein Riesling Grosses Gewächs, Rheinhessen

Located at Westhofen, this estate's Riesling wines come from three "grand cru" vineyards including Morstein, and the focus is, unusually, on dry styles. Morstein cru Riesling even in its youth shows great concentration, the result of intensive work in the vineyard and a gentle touch in the cellar.

Food pairings: White meat
Vintage years: 2007

9 Donnhoff, Oberhauser Bürcke Riesling Auslese Gold Cap, Nahe

This family have been making wine in the Nahe since 1750 and their wines have gained considerable respect. Featuring gray slate soils, they produce exemplary Rieslings—especially the 2007 late-harvest Auslese.

Food pairings: Medium-ripe cheeses and rich desserts
Vintage years: 2007

8 Emrich-Schönleber, Monzinger Halenberg Riesling Spätlese, Nahe

The Halenberg vineyard features very steep slopes facing south to southwest and vines grow on blue slate and quartzite soils. The grapes for this Spätlese are carefully selected and fermented slowly in stainless steel. Showing typical Halenberg spice and exotic fruit, this is a fine, fragrant wine.

Food pairings: Apple desserts, cheese, or savor on its own
Vintage years: 2007

10 Wirsching, Julius Echter Berg Silvaner Spätlese Trocken, Franconia

One of Franconia's leading estates, Wirsching's wines are made from a rich array of grapes lead by Silvaner along with Riesling, Müller-Thurgau, Weissburgunder, and Schaurebe. This wine is one of their finest, with an impressive spicy complexity.

Food pairings: Savor on its own
Vintage years: 2006

The "Rüdesheimer Berg Schlossberg" vineyard, Rüdesheim

Austria

Austria is best known for white wine; Grüner Veltliner steals the show, complemented by Welschriesling, Müller-Thurgau, Weissburgunder (Pinot Blanc), and Riesling. The styles, mostly dry and pure, have more affinity with Alsace than Germany. Thanks to the continental climate, they are generally full-bodied, potent, and made for food. The vineyards are located largely in the east and southeast of Austria; the regions most commonly found on labels are Wachau, Kremstal, Kamptal, and Burgenland. Austria's estates number around 20,000 and are often small, selling most wines at the cellar door or in nearby restaurants.

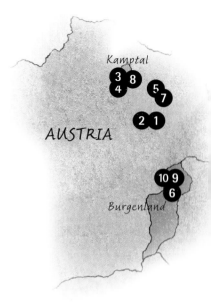

Golden vineyard with harvested grapes, Austria

1 Rainer Wess, Grüner Veltliner Wachauer, Wachau

Rainer Wess founded his winery in 2003 after extensive international experience. He sources the grapes for this wine from flat vineyards of Unterloiben and Dürnstein, where the gravelly, well-drained alluvial soils are well suited to Grüner Veltliner. The grapes are harvested early for this typical aromatic Wachau wine.

Food pairings: Cold meats or smoked fish
Vintage years: 2009, 2008, 2007

2 Rainer Wess Riesling Loibenberg, Wachau

The Loibenberg vineyard, where vines grown on ancient walled terraces, is one of Wachau's most scenic. This Riesling is dry, concentrated, with lovely texture. A minerally, savory character makes it an ideal food wine; with great cellaring potential, it will age gracefully.

Food pairings: Sea bass, monkfish, and other ocean fish
Vintage years: 2008, 2007

4 Hirsch Estate, Grüner Veltliner Heiligenstein, Kamptal

Family-run Hirsch Estate is in Kammern in the Kamp Valley overlooking the Heiligenstein and Gaisberg vineyards. Grapes are hand-picked and fermented with natural yeasts. The Grüner Veltliner is medium-bodied, with herbaceous notes.

Food pairings: Breaded or pan-fried white meat, asparagus
Vintage years: 2007, 2006

3 Jurtschitsch, Grüner Veltliner Dechant Alte Reben, Kamptal

Fruit for this wine is picked in late October from low-yielding old vines when the grapes are fully ripe. The wine ages on the lees and is bottled the spring after harvest. This is an unusually rich, full-bodied Grüner Veltliner, very versatile for food pairing.

Food pairings: Strongly flavored cheeses, braised beef
Vintage years: 2008, 2007

5 Weingut Bründlmayer, Riesling Zöbinger Heiligenstein

Bründlmayer has 22 acres of vineyards in the prime Zöbinger Heiligenstein area. In season, the vines are thinned to keep yields low. The must is fermented in stainless steel and matured in large vats for a short time, giving floral, peach, and citrus aromas.

Food pairings: Seafood, broiled fish, fried chicken, and schnitzel
Vintage years: 2007, 2006

6 Feiler-Artinger, Ruster Ausbruch Pinot Cuvée, Burgenland

A delightful wine made from Pinot Blanc, Pinot Gris, Neuburger, and Chardonnay grown around the town of Rust. Each variety is harvested separately, barrel-fermented, and aged in oak. Bright gold, its sweet and citrus flavors are balanced by fresh acidity. Elegant and long.

Food pairings: Blue cheeses; desserts
Vintage years: 2008, 2007

7 Weingut Bründlmayer, Grüner Veltliner Kamptaler Terrassen

The family-run winery at Langenlois offers an extensive wine range and a heuriger restaurant. This wine is a blend of wines sourced from various terraced vineyards, providing different characteristics; lime and apple fruit flavors, a slight herby character, and lively acidity.
Food pairings: Smoked trout; broiled fish
Vintage years: 2008, 2007

9 Kracher, Scheurebe TBA No.10, Swischen den Seen, Burgenland

Aromatic qualities and acidity make Scheurebe an ideal candidate for a TBA style with the ability to last years. Golden yellow, it has a long vinification of around 22 months to extract its full personality. Brimming with tropical and citrus fruit—a tooth-tingling wine.

Food pairings: Savor on its own
Vintage years: 2004

8 Schloss Gobelsburg, Grüner Veltliner Renner, Kamptal

This 86-acre estate is located on the slopes and terraces of old vineyard sites around Langenlois; Grüner Veltliner and Riesling wines are its specialty. The grapes for this Grüner Veltliner are picked early in the harvest to achieve its crisp freshness. Bone-dry and sophisticated.

Food pairings: Pork with rosti potatoes
Vintage years: 2009, 2008, 2007

10 Kracher, Grande Cuvée TBA No. 6 Nouvelle Vague, Burgenland

Nouvelle Vague wines are inspired by wine styles from around the world; the use of new oak and smaller barrels breaks Austrian tradition. A blend of Chardonnay and Welschriesling, this wine is complex and fruity. Enjoy now or cellar carefully.

Food pairings: Crème brulée
Vintage years: 2004

6   7   8   9   10

Vineyards in the commune of Rust, Burgenland

Hungary

Hungary is now one of the most interesting of the Eastern European wine-producing countries. Wines are produced in many areas of the country—most of it on the extensive vineyards of the Great Plain, but many more interesting wines come from hilly locations to the southwest and northeast. Vineyards around Lake Balaton are where other varieties perform well. However, the jewel in Hungary's crown is the Tokaji wines of Tokaj in the northeast. Here, ideal conditions produce exquisite sweet Aszú (noble rot) wines.

Botrytis-infected Furmint grapes, Tokaj

1 Dobogo Furmint, Tokaj

Made by Izabella Zwack, this wine is a blend of Furmint grapes from vineyards at Belsek in Mád and Palota in Tállya. The wine is partly aged in oak and partly in stainless steel. A dry, full-bodied wine with savory freshness on the palate. Try Dobogo's late harvest wines, too.

Food pairings: Smoked fish and white meats
Vintage years: 2008, 2007

2 Oremus, Tokaji Noble Late Harvest Furmint sw

Tokaji wines have been produced at Oremus since 1620. Today the winery facility is completely modern and owned by a Spanish consortium, and Oremus wines are highly respected. This is a medium-bodied, gently oaked wine with delightful apricot and honey flavors, finely tuned sweetness, acidity, and alcohol.

Food pairings: Enjoy a glass on its own instead of eating dessert
Vintage years: 2005

4 Királyudvar Winery, Tokaji Aszú 6 Puttonyos sw

This wine is made from around two-thirds Furmint and one-third Hárslevel. The botrytized grapes come from Királyudvar's prime Danczka vineyard. Fermentation takes place in Hungarian oak, then 42 months barrel-aging. Lovely orange blossom, honeyed fruit, and layered complexity.

Food pairings: Cake, peaches, or on its own
Vintage years: 2003, 2002

3 Disznók, 4 Puttonyos Tokaji Aszú sw 🛢

The Disznók estate has a privileged location in the southwest of the Tokaj-Hegyalja foothills, where most of its vineyards have a southerly aspect. Its wines range from dry Furmint to sweet wines and include the classic golden Aszú with spicy citrus notes and a zesty freshness. Enjoy now or cellar carefully.

Food pairings: Foie gras
Vintage years: 2004, 2001

5 The Royal Tokaji Wine Company, Tokaji Mezes Maly sw 🛢

Now owned by an Anglo-Hungarian consortium, this producer played a major role in Tokaji's renaissance. Over half its vineyards have a special cru classification, making wines with four puttonyos or more. This wine, with six, is concentrated and silky. An exquisite wine.

Food pairings: Foie gras
Vintage years: 1999

Slovenia

Located between the Adriatic and the Pannonian Plain, Slovenia's rolling foothills are ideal vine sites. Wines have been enjoyed by Western Europe for years, gaining international acclaim. There are three main regions: Primorska on the Adriatic, Posavje by the River Sava, and Podravje to the east, with a more continental climate. Primorska, bordering Italy's Friuli is the most exciting of the three. Its climate is influenced by both the coast and the Alps to the north. White grapes typically include Laski Rizling (Welschriesling), Sipon (Furmint), Ribolla Gialla (Rebula), and Renski Rizling (Rhine Riesling). Chardonnay, Sauvignon Blanc, Pinot varieties, and Gewürztraminer can also be found.

SLOVENIA
● Ljubljana

Rich, green vines in Jeruzalem

1 Verus Vineyards Furmint, Stajerska

Verus Vineyards was founded in 2007 by three young winemakers to produce fine white Slovenian wines from this eastern cool-climate area. Their Fermint is stainless-steel fermented and aged on the lees in new oak barrels. Herbaceous with a delightful silky texture, pure, fresh, and long. A delicious wine.

Food pairings: White fish and all kinds of poultry
Vintage years: 2009, 2008, 2007

2 Vinska Klet, Quercus Pinot Bianco, Goriska Brda

The grapes for this wine come from vineyards in the west close to the Adriatic. Most of the wine was fermented in stainless steel; a small amount was fermented and aged in French oak for complexity. Elegant and full-bodied with grapefruit and crisp apple fruit flavors.

Food pairings: Risotto and creamy pasta dishes
Vintage years: 2009, 2008

4 Movia Lunar, Goriska Brda

The Movia estate at Ceglo, bordering Italy, includes some prime. Its Lunar wine is made according to biodynamic methods from late harvest Rebula (Ribolla Gialla) grapes, which are fermented for eight months. An unusual wine with hints of pepper, lemongrass, and orange peel.

Food pairings: Broiled white fish
Vintage years: 2008, 2007

3 Cotar Malvazija, Kras Valley

This family-run vineyard, located close to the coast at Gorjansko, respects tradition and makes wines in ancient cellars carved out of rock. All its wines are fermented in oak with local yeasts. Its Malvazija (Malvasia) is aged for about two years in oak and bottled unfiltered. Dry, full-bodied, lively, and long.

Food pairings: White fish, lamb, chicken stew, medium-matured cheese
Vintage years: 2006, 2005

5 Marjan Simcic, Rebula Selekcija, Goriska Brda

Located in the region bordering Italy (Simcic's vineyards lie in both countries), this producer has 45 acres of 10- to 56-year-old vines. Made using traditional methods, this wine matures in large oak casks, giving it good structure and rich citrus flavor.

Food pairings: Soup, dishes with truffles, broiled fish
Vintage years: 2007, 2006

ENGLAND

London

GREECE

Athens

LEBANON

Beirut

Jerusalem

ISRAEL

The rest of the world

Climate change, social change, and greater prosperity are factors influencing wine production globally. More and better wine is being produced today in a surprisingly diverse set of countries as far apart as England and Thailand.

In China, the wine scene is evolving rapidly as a new generation takes to it, especially red wine. Most of the activity centers on the eastern Shandong Peninsula, which offers good potential thanks to its maritime climate and many south-facing slopes. China's best-known wines include Dragon Seal and Great Wall.

Japan's climate is far more challenging for wine production—typhoons tend to arrive just when vines need plenty of sun—yet a wine industry has been present here on a significant scale for over a century. It centers on the Yamanashi area near Tokyo, home to producers including Suntory, Grace, and Katsunuma.

Encouraged by a growing middle class, India has a prosperous wine scene pioneered by producers such as Château Indage and Sula, both located in the state of Maharashtra—a popular location for many Indian wine producers. The best vineyard sites are located in higher areas to combat low latitude.

Thailand also has a small number of producers including Château de Loei. The approach to winemaking is increasingly serious here and European grape varieties, including Chenin Blanc and Syrah, have been introduced.

In the following pages the white wines of England, Israel, Lebanon, and Greece are featured. Each of them has a distinctive wine style to offer.

England

In the early Middle Ages, the monastic vineyards of England were extensive and successful despite the all too elusive warm sunny fall needed to ripen grapes. The modern-day wine industry focuses on the southern half of England (and Wales), where there are a surprising number of small vineyards. Many of them are also well equipped to welcome visitors, especially in the counties of Kent, Sussex, and Surrey. White wines are far more important than red and are generally made from Germanic grapes such as Seyval Blanc, Reichensteiner, Müller-Thurgau, and Bacchus. Wine styles tend to offer very manageable alcohol levels, crisp acidity, and a distinctive aromatic style.

A vineyard of newly planted vines in Kent

1 Nyetimber Classic Cuvée, West Sussex Sp

Nyetimber was the first to show England's potential for traditional method sparkling wine based on the Champagne grapes. All the cuvées made at its estate in West Sussex are aged at least three years on the lees. Its Chardonnay-based Classic Cuvée has honey and citrus flavors and a toasty complexity.

Food matches: Smoked salmon blinis
Vintage years: 2003, 2001

2 Ridgeview Merret Bloomsbury, West Sussex Sp

Ridgeview Estate's vineyards are planted on the chalk/clay soils of the Sussex Downs. The particularly fine Merret cuvée is made from around 60 percent Chardonnay supported by Pinot Noir and Pinot Meunier for depth of flavor. A crisp sparkling wine to enjoy now or keep for a year or two.

Food matches: Duck pâté
Vintage years: 2006, 2005, 2004

4 Chapel Down Winery, Bacchus NV, Kent

With grapes from Kent and Essex, winemaker Owen Elias makes this wine, part of an impressive range of still and sparkling wines, at the sizeable Chapel Down Winery. No oak is used, just cold fermentation in stainless steel to achieve a fresh, fragrant, and versatile wine.

Food matches: A refreshing apéritif wine
Vintage years: NV

3 Hush Heath Estate, Balfour Brut Rosé, Kent R Sp

This delightful rosé sparkling wine, a relative newcomer to the sparkling wine scene, comes from vineyards in Kent attached to a Tudor manor. Owen Elias of English Wines Group makes the cuvée, an extremely fine wine with a hint of red currant fruit, perfectly balanced acidity, and an elegant creamy texture.

Food matches: A special wine to enjoy on its own
Vintage years: 2008, 2005, 2004

5 Denbies Wine Estate, Denbies Surrey Gold

A blend of Müller-Thurgau, Bacchus, and Ortega, this wine is a good introduction to English wine and the wide range offered by Denbies, one of England's largest and best-known estates. An unoaked wine with plenty of character, good fruit, and a hint of spice. Chill well.

Food matches: Salads, cold meats
Vintage years: 2008, 2007

Greece

As a wine-producing country, Greece finds itself at a crossroads. It has many wonderful indigenous grapes, but it's easier to rely on the broad appeal of international grapes in order to get a foothold in overseas markets. Greek producers make wonderful Chardonnay, Semillon, and even Sauvignon Blanc, but the glory lies in the mineral splendor of Santorini's Assyrtiko, the aromatic charms of the Peloponnese's Moschophilero, and the heady perfume of Macedonia's Malagousia. Greece also makes great sweet wines (look for Muscats and Vin Santo), and the occasional vibrantly flavored rosé.

Church among vineyards on Santorini

1 Tselepos, Moschophilero, Mantinia

Yiannis Tselepos is widely considered to be the king of Moschophilero, one of Greece's native grape varieties. His vineyards are planted in Mantinia, the grape's home ground. Moschophilero imparts flavors of spice and rose petals to the wine, which is often tinged with a rosy hue.

Food matches: Asian dishes
Vintage years: 2008, 2007

2 Domaine Sigalas, Assyrtiko, Santorini

The volcanic soils of the island of Santorini create the ideal conditions for growing Assyrtiko, Greece's emblematic white grape variety. The intense minerality of this wine can make it seem austere in its youth, but it mellows with time to take on a honeyed tone.

Food matches: Shellfish or white fish, simply broiled
Vintage years: 2007, 2005, 2004

4 Domaine Gerovassiliou, Malagousia, Regional Wine of Epanomi

Gerovassiliou's estate overlooks the Aegean Sea. One of the pioneers of modern winemaking in northern Greece, he rescued this once-rare grape from obscurity. It is a very aromatic wine, with notes of lavender, and tangerine zest on the palate.

Food matches: Sea bass
Vintage years: 2007, 2006

3 Kir-Yianni, Akakies Rosé, Amyndeon ®

Kir-Yianni, a small estate in northern Greece, is focused on the production of the local red grape, Xinomavro (pronounced Ksee-no-mav-ro). This vivid pink wine is based on the grape and has its characteristic red cherry and berry fruit, along with the crisp crunch of pomegranate seeds. Best drunk young.

Food matches: Barbecued salmon or tuna, charcuterie
Vintage years: 2008

5 Argyros, Vin Santo, Santorini ⓢⓦ

Argyros' Vin Santo is, arguably, Greece's most coveted dessert wine. Based on Santorini's own grape variety, Assyrtiko, with some Aidani and Athiri in the blend, the wine is aged for close to 20 years in barrel, by which time it has developed intense flavors of figs, dates, and toffee.

Food pairings: Why bother? Sip this instead of having dessert
Vintage years: 1986, 1984

Israel & Lebanon

The hills and plains of Lebanon and Israel were producing wine at a time when much of Western Europe was still drinking watery beer. By the 20th century, however, the fame of their vineyards had been largely eclipsed by the Middle East conflict. Amid all the struggles, the region's wine producers have started making a name for their increasingly good wines. Lebanon's wineries are concentrated in the Bekaa Valley, a high-altitude zone that lies to the north of the country's border with Israel. Israel's best wineries are concentrated in the Golan Heights, the Galilee, and the Judean Hills.

Grape-picking season at the Massaya vineyard in Bekaa Valley

① Massaya, Silver Selection White, Bekaa Valley, Lebanon

Massaya is among the finest producers of wine in Lebanon's Bekaa Valley. Its Silver Selection White, an unusual blend of 70 percent Sauvignon Blanc and 30 percent Chardonnay, is partially vinified and aged in oak to give it some textural weight to add to the Sauvignon-derived aromatics.

Food pairings: Sea bass stuffed with herbs
Vintage years: 2006, 2005

② Château Kefraya, Vissi d'Arte, Bekaa Valley, Lebanon

Vissi d'Arte is a new wine for Château Kefraya, one of Lebanon's premium producers. The vineyards are planted at high altitude, which gives this exotic and aromatic blend of Viognier and Chardonnay lively acidity and heady aromatics. Barrel aging adds a spicy richness.

Food matches: Mildly spiced Asian dishes, sushi
Vintage years: 2006

④ Dalton, Sauvignon Blanc Fumé, Upper Galilee, Israel

Based in an industrial park in the Upper Galilee, Mat Haruni's winery has become a consistent source of quality, reasonably priced wines. This kosher wine, made from lightly oaked Sauvignon Blanc, has generous, ripe fruit on the palate.

Food matches: Thai seafood stir-fries
Vintage years: 2008

③ Clos de Gat, Chardonnay, Judean Hills, Israel

Clos de Gat is a joint project of Kibbutz Har'el and winemaker Eyal Rotem. The winery has been up and running for less than a decade but it's already become a byword for quality reds and whites. Its award-winning Chardonnay is richly fruited, with a creamy texture, and a generous finish.

Food matches: Roast chicken with vegetables
Vintage years: 2007, 2006, 2005

⑤ Domaine du Castel, Blanc du Castel, 'C' Chardonnay, Judean Hills, Israel

Inspired by France's classic wines, Eli Ben Zaken produced his first vintage of 600 bottles back in 1992. He's now acknowledged as a pioneer of Israel's boutique winemaking movement. His richly oaked Chardonnay has ripe fruit flavors, with a balancing acidity.

Food matches: Turbot or monkfish
Vintage years: 2007, 2005

index

picture credits

The images in this book are used with the permission of the copyright holders stated below. (Images are listed by page number.) All other illustrations and pictures are copyright of Quintet Publishing Limited. While every effort has been made to credit contributors, Quintet would like to apologize should there have been any omissions or errors and would be pleased to make the appropriate correction for future editions of the book.

5 Faber, Armin / Stockfood; 7 Koeb, Ulrike / Stockfood America; 8 Ferroni, Laura / Stockfood America; 12 New, Myles / Stockfood America; 17 Lehmann, Jörg / Stockfood America; 19 Faber, Armin / Stockfood America; 23 Lehmann, Jörg / Stockfood America; 24 Faber, Armin / Stockfood America; 25 Faber, Armin / Stockfood America; 27 Lehmann, Herbert / Stockfood America; 29 Faber, Armin / Stockfood America; 30 Carriere, James / Stockfood America; 33 Morris, Steven / Stockfood America; 37 Morris, Steven / Stockfood America; 39 Vasseur, Frederic / Stockfood America; 41 Williams, Paul / Stockfood America; 42 Czap, Daniel / Stockfood America; 45 Carriere, James / Stockfood America; 46 Rupp Tina / Stockfood America; 56 Holler, Hendrik / Stockfood America; 58 Faber, Armin / Stockfood America; 61 Morris, Steven / Stockfood America; 62 Faber, Armin / Stockfood America; 65 Faber, Armin / Stockfood America; 66 Shutterstock; 70 Holler, Hendrick / Stockfood America; 72 Holler, Hendrik / Stockfood America; 75 Morris, Steven / Stockfood America; 76 Holler, Hendrik / Stockfood America; 79 Faber, Armin / Stockfood America; 80 Shutterstock; 86 Faber, Armin / Stockfood America; 88 Holler, Hendrik / Stockfood America; 91 Siffert, Hans–Peter / Stockfood America; 92 Holler, Hendrik / Stockfood America; 96 Holler, Hendrik / Stockfood America; 99 Holler, Hendrik / Stockfood America; 100 Faber, Armin / Stockfood America; 102 Gandara, Fernando / Stockfood America; 108 Siffert, Hans–Peter / Stockfood America; 110 Morris, Steven / Stockfood America; 112 Holler, Hendrik / Stockfood America; 114 Morris, Steven / Stockfood America; 116 Morris, Steven / Stockfood America; 120 Morris, Steven / Stockfood America; 122 Siffert, Hans–Peter / Stockfood America; 125 Holler, Hendrik / Stockfood America; 128 Siffert, Hans–Peter / Stockfood; 130 Siffert, Hans–Peter / Stockfood America; 132 Holler, Hendrik / Stockfood America; 134 Holler, Hendrik / Stockfood America; 136 Faber, Armin / Stockfood America; 140 Holler, Hendrik / Stockfood America; 143 Holler, Hendrik / Stockfood America; 144 Holler, Hendrik / Stockfood America; 146 Holler, Hendrik / Stockfood America; 148 Faber, Armin / Stockfood America; 152 Faber, Armin / Stockfood America; 156 Lehmann, Jörg / FoodCollection / Stockfood America; 159 Siffert, Hans–Peter / Stockfood America; 160 Lehmann, Jörg / Stockfood America; 164 shutterstock; 167 Siffert, Hans–Peter / Stockfood America; 168 Faber, Armin / Stockfood America; 171 Lehmann, Jörg / Stockfood America; 172 Siffert, Hans–Peter / Stockfood America; 174 Siffert, Hans–Peter / Stockfood America; 178 Lehmann, Jörg / Stockfood America; 181 Shutterstock; 183 Faber, Armin / Stockfood America; 184 Lehmann, Jörg / Stockfood America; 187 Morris, Steven / Stockfood America; 188 Holler, Hendrik / Stockfood America; 190 Lehmann, Jörg / Stockfood America; 193 Siffert, Hans–Peter / Stockfood America; 194 Siffert, Hans–Peter / Stockfood America; 196 Lehmann, Jörg / Stockfood America; 198 Holler, Hendrik / Stockfood America; 202 Lehmann, Jörg / Stockfood America; 205 Morris, Steven / Stockfood America; 208 Shutterstock; 210 Shutterstock; 212 Siffert, Hans–Peter / Stockfood America; 216 Siffert, Hans–Peter / Stockfood America; 218 Faber, Armin / Stockfood America; 221 Faber, Armin / Stockfood America; 222 Holler, Hendrik / Stockfood America; 225 Holler, Hendrik / Stockfood America; 226 Siffert, Hans–Peter / Stockfood America; 229 Holler, Hendrik / Stockfood America; 232 Faber, Armin / Stockfood America; 235 Morris, Steven / Stockfood America; 236 Holler, Hendrik / Stockfood America; 239 Holler, Hendrik / Stockfood America; 240 Holler, Hendrik / Stockfood America; 243 Holler, Hendrik / Stockfood America; 244 Holler, Hendrik / Stockfood America; 246 Faber, Armin / Stockfood America; 248 Morris, Steven / Stockfood America; 250 Faber, Armin / Stockfood America; 256 Holler, Hendrik / Stockfood America; 259 Holler, Hendrik / Stockfood America; 260 Faber, Armin / Stockfood America; 262 Weber, Inge / Stockfood America; 265 Holler, Hendrik / Stockfood America; 266 Lehmann, Herbert / Stockfood America; 269 Faber, Armin / Stockfood America; 270 Lehmann, Herbert / Stockfood America; 272 Faber, Armin / Stockfood America; 276 Shutterstock; 278 Grilly, Bernard / Stockfood America; 280 Massaya & Co.

acknowledgments

The authors would like to thank contributors Christine Austin, Jim Budd, and Wink Lorch.

Quintet would like to thank the following wine agencies and vineyards who helped with the wine bottle image research in the book: ABS Wines; Accent Communications; Bibendum Wine; Boutinot Limited; Calera Wines; Chateau Musar; Clark Foyster Wines Ltd; Domaine de Poumeyrade; Enotria Wines; Fells; Felton Road; Freixenet; Fields Morris Verdin Wines; François Lurton; Genesis Wines; Great Western Wine; H&H Bancroft Wines; Hallgarten; Inniskillin Wines; Las Bodegas; Layment & Shaw Wine Merchants; La Sauvageonne; Lea & Sandeman Co. Ltd; Les Caves de Pyrene; Liberty Wines; Limm Communications; Maison Sichel; Moet Hennessey; Menztendorff; Morgan Winery; Moreno Wines; Négociants; Patriarche Wines; Pol Roger; Raymond Reynolds Ltd; Richards Walford & Company; Schloss Gobelsburg; Seckford Agencies; The Real Wine Company; Thorman Hunt & Co; Vickbar Wine; Wine Partners; Wine Treasury; Yvon Mau.

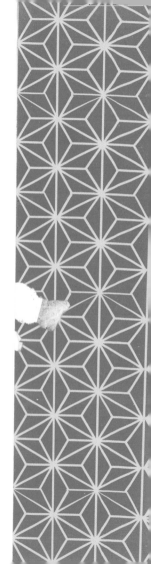

picture credits

The images in this book are used with the permission of the copyright holders stated below. (Images are listed by page number.) All other illustrations and pictures are copyright of Quintet Publishing Limited. While every effort has been made to credit contributors, Quintet would like to apologize should there have been any omissions or errors and would be pleased to make the appropriate correction for future editions of the book.

5 Faber, Armin / Stockfood; 7 Koeb, Ulrike / Stockfood America; 8 Ferroni, Laura / Stockfood America; 12 New, Myles / Stockfood America; 17 Lehmann, Jörg / Stockfood America; 19 Faber, Armin / Stockfood America; 23 Lehmann, Jörg / Stockfood America; 24 Faber, Armin / Stockfood America; 25 Faber, Armin / Stockfood America; 27 Lehmann, Herbert / Stockfood America; 29 Faber, Armin / Stockfood America; 30 Carriere, James / Stockfood America; 33 Morris, Steven / Stockfood America; 37 Morris, Steven / Stockfood America; 39 Vasseur, Frederic / Stockfood America; 41 Williams, Paul / Stockfood America; 42 Czap, Daniel / Stockfood America; 45 Carriere, James / Stockfood America; 46 Rupp Tina / Stockfood America; 56 Holler, Hendrik / Stockfood America; 58 Faber, Armin / Stockfood America; 61 Morris, Steven / Stockfood America; 62 Faber, Armin / Stockfood America; 65 Faber, Armin / Stockfood America; 66 Shutterstock; 70 Holler, Hendrick / Stockfood America; 72 Holler, Hendrik / Stockfood America; 75 Morris, Steven / Stockfood America; 76 Holler, Hendrik / Stockfood America; 79 Faber, Armin / Stockfood America; 80 Shutterstock; 86 Faber, Armin / Stockfood America; 88 Holler, Hendrik / Stockfood America; 91 Siffert, Hans-Peter / Stockfood America; 92 Holler, Hendrik / Stockfood America; 96 Holler, Hendrik / Stockfood America; 99 Holler, Hendrik / Stockfood America; 100 Faber, Armin / Stockfood America; 102 Gandara, Fernando / Stockfood America; 108 Siffert, Hans-Peter / Stockfood America; 110 Morris, Steven / Stockfood America; 112 Holler, Hendrik / Stockfood America; 114 Morris, Steven / Stockfood America; 116 Morris, Steven / Stockfood America; 120 Morris, Steven / Stockfood America; 122 Siffert, Hans-Peter / Stockfood America; 125 Holler, Hendrik / Stockfood America; 128 Siffert, Hans-Peter / Stockfood; 130 Siffert, Hans-Peter / Stockfood America; 132 Holler, Hendrik / Stockfood America; 134 Holler, Hendrik / Stockfood America; 136 Faber, Armin / Stockfood America; 140 Holler, Hendrik / Stockfood America; 143 Holler, Hendrik / Stockfood America; 144 Holler, Hendrik / Stockfood America; 146 Holler, Hendrik / Stockfood America; 148 Faber, Armin / Stockfood America; 152 Faber, Armin / Stockfood America; 156 Lehmann, Jörg / FoodCollection / Stockfood America; 159 Siffert, Hans-Peter / Stockfood America; 160 Lehmann, Jörg / Stockfood America; 164 shutterstock; 167 Siffert, Hans-Peter / Stockfood America; 168 Faber, Armin / Stockfood America; 171 Lehmann, Jörg / Stockfood America; 172 Siffert, Hans-Peter / Stockfood America; 174 Siffert, Hans-Peter / Stockfood America; 178 Lehmann, Jörg / Stockfood America; 181 Shutterstock; 183 Faber, Armin / Stockfood America; 184 Lehmann, Jörg / Stockfood America; 187 Morris, Steven / Stockfood America; 188 Holler, Hendrik / Stockfood America; 190 Lehmann, Jörg / Stockfood America; 193 Siffert, Hans-Peter / Stockfood America; 194 Siffert, Hans-Peter / Stockfood America; 196 Lehmann, Jörg / Stockfood America; 198 Holler, Hendrik / Stockfood America; 202 Lehmann, Jörg / Stockfood America; 205 Morris, Steven / Stockfood America; 208 Shutterstock; 210 Shutterstock; 212 Siffert, Hans-Peter / Stockfood America; 216 Siffert, Hans-Peter / Stockfood America; 218 Faber, Armin / Stockfood America; 221 Faber, Armin / Stockfood America; 222 Holler, Hendrik / Stockfood America; 225 Holler, Hendrik / Stockfood America; 226 Siffert, Hans-Peter / Stockfood America; 229 Holler, Hendrik / Stockfood America; 232 Faber, Armin / Stockfood America; 235 Morris, Steven / Stockfood America; 236 Holler, Hendrik / Stockfood America; 239 Holler, Hendrik / Stockfood America; 240 Holler, Hendrik / Stockfood America; 243 Holler, Hendrik / Stockfood America; 244 Holler, Hendrik / Stockfood America; 246 Faber, Armin / Stockfood America; 248 Morris, Steven / Stockfood America; 250 Faber, Armin / Stockfood America; 256 Holler, Hendrik / Stockfood America; 259 Holler, Hendrik / Stockfood America; 260 Faber, Armin / Stockfood America; 262 Weber, Inge / Stockfood America; 265 Holler, Hendrik / Stockfood America; 266 Lehmann, Herbert / Stockfood America; 269 Faber, Armin / Stockfood America; 270 Lehmann, Herbert / Stockfood America; 272 Faber, Armin / Stockfood America; 276 Shutterstock; 278 Grilly, Bernard / Stockfood America; 280 Massaya & Co.

acknowledgments

The authors would like to thank contributors Christine Austin, Jim Budd, and Wink Lorch.

Quintet would like to thank the following wine agencies and vineyards who helped with the wine bottle image research in the book: ABS Wines; Accent Communications; Bibendum Wine; Boutinot Limited; Calera Wines; Chateau Musar; Clark Foyster Wines Ltd; Domaine de Poumeyrade; Enotria Wines; Fells; Felton Road; Freixenet; Fields Morris Verdin Wines; François Lurton; Genesis Wines; Great Western Wine; H&H Bancroft Wines; Hallgarten; Inniskillin Wines; Las Bodegas; Layment & Shaw Wine Merchants; La Sauvageonne; Lea & Sandeman Co. Ltd; Les Caves de Pyrene; Liberty Wines; Limm Communications; Maison Sichel; Moet Hennessey; Menztendorff; Morgan Winery; Moreno Wines; Négociants; Patriarche Wines; Pol Roger; Raymond Reynolds Ltd; Richards Walford & Company; Schloss Gobelsburg; Seckford Agencies; The Real Wine Company; Thorman Hunt & Co; Vickbar Wine; Wine Partners; Wine Treasury; Yvon Mau.

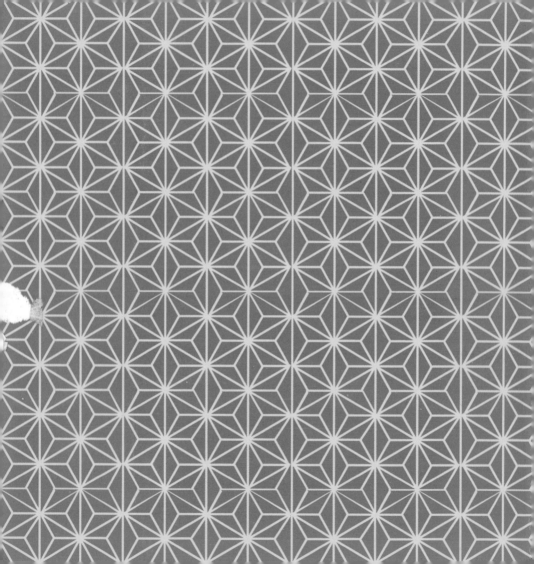